DIPS, DISRUPTIONS
& DESTINY

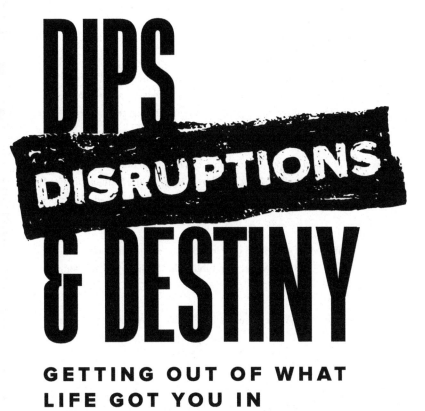

DIPS DISRUPTIONS & DESTINY

GETTING OUT OF WHAT LIFE GOT YOU IN

DAVID HAWKINS

DIPS, DISRUPTIONS & DESTINY
17 Gateway Drive
Collinsville, IL 62234

ISBN 978-0-578-90668-3
First Edition 2021

Design: Lydia Tarleton
Printed in the United States of America 2021

ENDORSEMENTS

"Some earthquakes shake the foundation and structures of the earth's material ground. But then there are lifequakes that shake, shape, and form our truest character. Pastor David Hawkins, a master orator and anointed spiritual carpenter, puts his life lessons on display in his new book: *Dips, Disruptions & Destiny*. I encourage everyone to get it, study it, and allow your life to be spiritually and intellectually transformed."

Apostle Carlos Malone
The Bethel Church | Miami, FL

"David has written a must-read road map for anyone considering deepening their faith journey. Read this book and learn from one of this generation's most dynamic leaders. Trust me, *Dips, Disruptions & Destiny* is for you."

Anthony Meyers
Pastor & Author of "1440 - Minutes Matter When Living an Intentional Life"

To my parents, Matthew Lee & Hazel Hawkins, my heroes! You all sacrificed so much for us as kids. From the missed meals so that we could eat, to the lathering of love to insulate our dreams. It's because of your fortitude we get to do this.

CONTENTS

FOREWORD

BY RANDALL LITTLETON

I met David 15 years ago. At the time, he was a pharmaceutical sales rep. He spent his days traveling around the region and the evenings pastoring a church. What impressed me the most was his commitment to pastoring his congregation. It's not an easy calling to pastor a church—especially when you have limited time and resources. But David did—and he did so with passion. It was easy to tell that he loved the people of Living the Word Church and had a heart for seeing God do amazing things in the St. Louis region.

Over the next 15 years, David was able to quit his day job and transition to become a full-time pastor. He and I met every week in those early years. We talked strategy. We talked about vision. We talked about the power of God moving. We talked about seeing a region change. I had a front-row seat to what God was doing in and through David and Living the Word Church. Our churches began to partner with each other. I watched as God grew Living the Word from a congregation of around 30 to 100. Then to 300. Then to 500. And now to over 800. God was, and is, truly up to something.

There's something exciting about seeing God at work. I marvel at seeing lives change, marriages saved, and cycles of generational sin being redeemed. But even with those stories, pastoring a church isn't easy. For every story of God at work, there seems to also be a story of heartache…of trouble. Crisis is always just around the corner. It's sometimes easy for a pastor to hide the dips and disruptions of life. It's tempting to pretend they don't exist. It can be difficult for a pastor to admit that there is trouble, especially personal trouble, out loud. It is a lonely place to be.

That's why I can't wait for you to dive into this book. In Dips, Disruptions, and Destiny, you will see what it looks like to walk a refreshingly authentic journey of faith. You will learn from David's life, as well as the Old Testament hero of the faith, Joshua. While this book will serve pastors and leaders well, it is really for anyone who experiences dips and disruptions. The practical and theological applications will give you hope and encouragement. Through it all, you will see that God is good and He is faithful.

Faithful. God is faithful. That's what you will see in this book. You will also see a life that clings to the steadfast faithfulness of God. I am a better pastor, father, and husband because of David and his friendship. I can't wait for you to have the front row seat that I have been blessed to have over the years.

ONE

LIFEQUAKES

I wish I was dead.

I drove home from church slowly, walked through the door of my new rental house, and felt like a foreigner in my own residence. None of my personal belongings were there to make me feel at home, and most of the rooms were still empty. Worst of all, my son wasn't there to run into my arms, and that's what made me feel the most empty. I was an empty man in an empty house.

I plopped down on a brown couch I had just purchased. It was there that the most terrifying thoughts I've ever experienced played through my head. My thoughts guided my hands, and before I knew it, I was carelessly fumbling around with my firearm.

I had never been in such an intense battle with the Evil One. It felt like we were in a forty-eight-round boxing match, even though it only lasted about ten minutes. During those ten minutes, I struggled spiritually, emotionally, and physically like never before. For the first time ever, the temptation to take my life was far greater than the will to go on. The Devil hijacked my thoughts and continuously reminded me of destructive words that had been spoken over my life. They had come from people who I thought really loved me.

You'll never survive this. You're going to die.

It was hard to fathom how I had gotten to this place of extreme distress. From the outside looking in, my life seemed pretty well put together. I was the pastor of a growing church, a proud father, and had built a beautiful home with my wife. But things are not always what they seem on the surface. A few weeks before battling suicidal thoughts on my brown couch, the bottom of my life fell out completely. That's when my wife and I stood before the church and announced that we were getting a divorce.

The truth is, our marriage didn't suddenly and unexpectedly fall apart one day. It was a troubled marriage from the jump and continued to grow worse over time. We participated in extensive counseling for eight years, which unfortunately didn't help whatsoever. There was no scandal, abuse, misappropriation of money, or major sin issues that tore us apart. However, I found out about some extremely toxic and disrespectful things that were happening behind my back. I knew the only way to salvage both of our futures was to go our separate ways.

I suppose we could have hidden behind the facade of respectable pastor and first lady for a little bit longer. Fake smiles can convince people for a while, but I knew myself, and I'm too real to pretend. Even though it was going to be hard, we needed to be transparent with the people who were following us.

No pastor ever wants to stand in front of his church and announce his divorce. As you can imagine, the Pharisaical crowd began to pick up rocks to throw at me. Not only did they try to tear me apart, they tried to tear the church apart as well. They recruited others to join in the fight of slandering my reputation and over-powering my authority. I'm thankful for the church members who chose to love me in the middle of my lowest moment. Still, there was an obvious division that started to build within the church.

Two weeks after the announcement, I took the pulpit to preach on Sunday morning. In all honesty, preaching was the last thing in the world I felt like doing. My week had been filled with dodging rocks, extreme pressure, and an unbelievable number of uncomfortable conversations. I was trying to hold the church together while my personal life was falling apart. Nevertheless, I opened my Bible, grabbed the microphone, and prayed that useful words would come out of my mouth.

I had nothing to give the people, but God literally spoke through me. It was one of the most powerful services I'd ever experienced - healings and deliverances were breaking out all over the place. The presence of God was obviously there and people were hungry for Him. When I finished my sermon and walked away from the pulpit, people were still passionately praising and worshiping God. It was every preacher's dream!

As I made my way to the back of the room, I walked past church members who had hands lifted in worship and tears running down their faces. They were feeling God's love, grace, and goodness in a tangible way. Meanwhile, all I could feel was the emptiness on the inside of me. Before I left the room, I muttered beneath my breath: "I hate this sh—."

I know, I know. That sounds like a pretty rough thing for a preacher to say. But it's genuinely how I felt at that moment. The reality of the separation hit me, fear of losing my son haunted me, the embarrassment of divorce weighed on me, and anger toward God consumed me.

As I watched God put the lives of others back together, I knew that mine was in the process of falling apart. I didn't fully know how to digest all of it, but I was confident of one thing: whatever God was doing for them, He surely wasn't doing for me.

The reality I preached about was starkly different than the one I drove home to that day. On the way, I wondered if I was a hypocrite - which is a word that I can't stand. In my distraught state, I couldn't help but feel I had lied to our church. I had lost confidence in the God I preached about so confidently.

Everything came to a head when I plopped down on that couch with my gun in hand. I felt like I had tried my best to do everything right. I gave my life to preach the Gospel, I served people, I prayed fervently, and I stayed away from sin. But somehow, when it came to marriage, things went very, very wrong.

I failed in public. I failed in private. I failed as a pastor. I failed as a husband. Worst of all, I failed as a father.

I was certain I had done everything right, and it still didn't work.

FAIRY TALES & LIFEQUAKES

That day was inevitably the toughest of my life - and I'm a man who has been through a lot. I grew up in the hood and understand what struggle feels like. But on that day, my story was totally sabotaged. It suddenly felt like my fairy tale got hijacked.

Fairy tales aren't necessarily just for children. The truth is that we all have a fairy tale version of the life we're chasing. Typically, our rationale does a pretty decent job of reminding us that picture-perfect lives are unrealistic and unattainable, but reality doesn't completely diminish desire. I hoped for a version of life in which I'd be viewed as the perfect pastor, husband, and father. I wanted to create the legacy of a man who didn't come from much but made much of himself and his family.

Maybe your fairy tale is still very much alive, or perhaps it's buried underneath layers of doubt and discouragement. Unfortunately, our stories never seem to go exactly as we think they should. Life has a way of providing us with all sorts of challenges, failures, and disappointments.

For me, it was divorce. For you, it might be something completely different: sickness, career failure, moral mistakes, or the loss of someone close to you. Please, don't hear me wrong! I'm not wishing for any of those things to happen to you. But as a pastor, I do feel an obligation to prepare you for how to respond if and when they do. How will you react when your fairy tale is hijacked by life?

Maybe you aren't buying into this whole fairy tale idea! Maybe you're a "realist" or you've already given up on perfect because of the hurt you've experienced. You might be saying, "I'm past the fairy tale stage-of-life, you better come preaching better than that!" Here are some reflection questions for you, specifically:

- What happens when your planning gets side-tracked by mishaps and reversals?
- What happens when you forget the main purpose of life and get distracted by details?
- What happens when crap happens, and you don't know how to clean up the mess?

If you've experienced any of the above tensions, that means that you have faced, are facing, or will face disruptions. Disruptions are inconvenient, but we've also come to expect them. When the tires blow out on your car, you usually have a friend who can get you some at a discounted rate. If not, GoFundMe is always there for you! For the most part, we don't mind a disruption. We've become skilled and experienced at navigating one or two of them at a time. What we do mind is when four or five disruptions hold a strategic convention and pick our address as the house they're going to visit.

Don't you hate it when life throws a molotov cocktail of disruptions your way? Facing disruptions becomes increasingly challenging when it's not just one or two, but four or five that blitz you all at the same time. I'm talking about when you get hit with a handful of these whammies one after the other:

- Your daughter is failing seventh grade.
- Your job is in jeopardy.
- You might lose the house.
- You can't keep up with the car repairs.
- Your teenager won't stop partying.
- You were diagnosed with cancer.
- Your spouse was diagnosed with cancer.
- You don't have extra money to pay medical bills.
- Your parents are dying.

In his book, *Life Is in the Transitions*, Bruce Feiler defines these moments as "lifequakes."[1] A lifequake happens when the many stresses of life collide together and impact you at the very core of your being. Just as the core of the earth is shaken during an earthquake, the core of your life is shaken during a lifequake. There is no telling how long the shaking will last or how much destruction it will ultimately cause.

A couple of major disruptions strung together are enough to

shake the foundation of your humanity and spirituality. Sometimes, what you hoped would be a brief inconvenience ends up lasting much longer than anticipated. If you experience enough disruptions, you just might find yourself in what I call a dip - an extended period of being disoriented, destabilized, and depressed.

Disruptions and dips hijack fairy tales and ruin picture-perfect aspirations. Unfortunately, this book will not teach you how to avoid them. But through the Bible, we're going to put God on trial. What does that mean? Together, we will expose His character and press into what He's doing during our most desperate moments.

Up to this point, we've hit on some pretty heavy things. If you were to shut the pages of this book and put it back on the shelf now, you might find yourself feeling pretty discouraged. But I promise as we go along, we will find that life is not all bad. In fact, even when it is bad, God is still up to something good.

Throughout this book, I'm going to take my best shot at showing the magnitude of God's goodness by unpacking the rest of my story. My promise to you is this: I refuse to hide any of the nitty-gritty details, even the ones that are uncomfortably messy. Why? It is the depths of our garbage that define the depths of God's grace.

MEET JOSHUA

We're also about to adventure into the story of a man named Joshua. You might know him as the army general who marched his troops around Jericho, causing the walls of an entire city to collapse by faith alone. Or perhaps you recognize him as God's mighty warrior, who led the Israelites to victory in battle after battle upon entering the Promised Land.

But where we pick up in his story, we'll be introduced to a man who was on his last leg - someone who had experienced a pretty intense lifequake. We'll meet the Joshua who was disoriented, destabilized, despondent, and defeated.

IT IS THE DEPTHS OF OUR GARBAGE THAT DEFINE THE DEPTHS OF GOD'S GRACE.

In his story, we see two tensions exist simultaneously. Joshua was undoubtedly a man of destiny. But before he reached destiny, he experienced extreme disruptions and extensive dips. We tend to think that destiny and difficulty are mutually exclusive. However, in God's brilliance, he perfectly weaves the two tensions together to bring purpose and meaning out of every moment of life.

I have no clue what life has got you in, and maybe you have no idea how to get out. But let me leave you with one encouragement that I know, without a shadow of a doubt, to be 100-percent true: Through all of your dips and disruptions, God wants to *direct* you.

REFLECTION & APPLICATION

1. If your fairy tale version of life came true, how would it look?

2. What disruptions have you experienced en route to your fairy tale? How have you handled them?

3. How have the difficulties of life changed your view of God? Has your hope been damaged or diminished?

TWO

DRIPPING WITH DESTINY

If you would have told me that I'd someday contemplate ending my own life, I would have called you a liar. Nobody ever believes they're going to be *that* guy, and I certainly was no exception. Up to that point, such a drastic state of physical, mental, emotional, and spiritual darkness was not the narrative of my life. I think that's why I relate so much to Joshua.

Throughout this book, we will find a man who experienced severe disruptions and dips. Because of how life unfolded, Joshua battled extreme discouragement, and one might even argue he struggled with deep depression. But that's not where his story started. In fact, where Joshua ended up is diametrically opposed to where he began.

Joshua was no different than you and me. Before his existence on Earth officially began, God had an intricate, intentional plan for his life. Oftentimes, that plan doesn't go as smoothly as we'd hope. God doesn't always direct us *around* disruptions and dips, He directs us *through* them. And although things didn't unfold exactly how Joshua anticipated, from the time he was a young man, God's hand was on his life in a powerful way. He was what I refer to as *dripping with destiny*. I'll prove it to you as we dive into some Scripture.

It was Moses' practice to take the Tent of Meeting and set it up some distance from the camp. Everyone who wanted to make a request of the Lord would go to the Tent of Meeting outside the camp.

Whenever Moses went out to the Tent of Meeting, all the people would get up and stand in the entrances of their own tents. They would all watch Moses until he disappeared inside. As he went into the tent, the pillar of cloud would come down and hover at its entrance while the Lord spoke with Moses. When the people saw the cloud standing at the entrance of the tent, they would stand and bow down in front of their own tents. Inside the Tent of Meeting, the Lord would speak to Moses face to face, as one speaks to a friend. Afterward Moses would return to the camp, but the young man who

*assisted him, Joshua son of Nun, would remain behind in the Tent of
Meeting. (Exodus 33:7-11, NLT)*

Here, we enter the narrative of God's chosen people, the Israelites.
Through a man named Moses, God miraculously freed them from
slavery in the land of Egypt, where they had been held in captivity
for the last 400 years. His plan was to lead them into the Promised
Land, which flowed with milk and honey (Exodus 3:8). It was going
to be a far cry from the oppression to which they had grown so
accustomed.

In order to get to the Promised Land, God had to lead them
through the wilderness, in this case, the desert. It was a place where
they had to face their uncertainty and develop a dependency on
God. Although slavery was brutal, they were used to operating under
the control of others. Within the context of slavery came survival.
But in the wilderness, they had no idea where food or water would
come from. God used that context to teach them how to operate as
His children. How? He led them. Through His law, He gave them
healthy parameters to live by. Through His miraculous provision, He
became the source of their survival in the middle of a harsh climate.

During the Israelite's initial season of wilderness, we see their
leader, Moses, spending extended amounts of time in the presence
of God. There's no way to know for sure what the two of them were
talking about, but I know the many stresses of leadership all too well!
I'm certain that Moses was desperate for God to relieve the pressure
of leading thousands upon thousands of people into new territory.
Inevitably, having never been in those shoes before, he was searching
for guidance and wisdom on the best way to move forward.

Unlike today, the presence of God wasn't easily accessible to
everybody whenever, wherever. Instead, He would hang out in one
place, at one time. Specifically, during the wilderness expeditions,
God would manifest Himself as a pillar of cloud by day and a pillar
of fire by night (Exodus 13:21-22). It was His method of leading

His people in a way that was tangible to them. So whenever Moses wanted to meet with God, he would enter into a structure called the Tent of Meeting. The pillar of cloud would hover outside the entrance of the Tent, and God would speak with Moses inside, face to face.

The Tent of Meeting became exactly what its name implied - a meeting place. How incredible is it that whenever Moses wanted to talk to God, all he had to do was show up at their spot, and God would meet him there? Furthermore, inside of the Tent, they talked like friends. It was personal, it was authentic, and it was exclusive to Moses! Well, at least it was supposed to be.

Our subject of study, Joshua, would assist Moses wherever he went, rarely leaving his side. Moses was an older man and Joshua a younger one in comparison. The fact that Moses chose Joshua to be his right-hand-man shows there was extraordinary potential inside of him. Here we see that Joshua not only had potential to be used by God, but also a great hunger to be with God. Whenever Moses would finish up his one-on-one with God and go back to his own tent for the evening, Joshua would stay behind. Essentially, he would pick up where Moses left off.

What motivation did Joshua have to stay behind in the Tent? Again, there's no way for us to know for sure, but there was undoubtedly a reason Joshua wanted to stay. I can imagine him having a personal conversation with God, while angelic hosts were in their midst.

The truth is, Joshua was *lingering*. Have you ever had company over and that one person lingers around well past the time everybody else has left to go home? They might have something urgent to tell you. Or maybe they are desperate for one more conversation. Perhaps they just don't want to be alone. That's the picture we see of Joshua. He hung out past the time that any activity was supposed to be happening in the Tent. Moses had left, meaning that God was officially off the clock. But time and time again, we see Joshua lingering, hoping to have his moment in the presence of God.

The Hebrew word used to describe Joshua's tendency to "remain behind" or "linger" is the term "mush." And no; the translation of mush is not porridge, nor is it the English equivalent of being overly sentimental. It literally means to make the decision to not leave.[1]

We see the authors of the Bible use this concept numerous times throughout its many books. In fact, the term is first used to describe the pillar of cloud and fire. But in this case, instead of the Israelites choosing not to leave the presence of God, it was the presence of God choosing not to depart from the Israelites.

In the life of Jesus, many of his followers would leave Him after He taught on controversial topics or asked for deeper allegiance. On one such occasion, Jesus asked His closest disciples if they'd leave as well. Peter's response was mushy: "Lord, to whom would we go? You have the words that give eternal life. We believe, and we know you are the Holy One of God" (John 6:68-69). Peter made it abundantly clear that there was no better alternative. He basically said, "We've done the research and there's no better cause for us to follow. We've lingered long enough to believe in who You are because of the things we've seen You do. You aren't just some fleeting alternative; we've eliminated every other option. And because of that, we're sticking with you."

Unfortunately, most Christians will miss God repeatedly because they choose not to linger. When times get tough, they buckle and break. They may enter God's presence hopeful, but when He doesn't produce immediately, they instantly get up and try something else. If we ever want to see results, we must choose to be mushy.

It's easy to get annoyed when somebody gets mushy with us and overstays their welcome. But that's not the posture of God. Joshua lingered constantly because when he did, God stuck around consistently. A relationship with Him always goes two ways. When it comes to God's presence, He is willing to stay for as long as He is wanted. The more of God that Joshua experienced, the more of that experience he desired. The Bible tells us that in His presence there is "fullness of joy" (Psalm 16:11). After his time with God, I am sure that Joshua left with an overwhelming joyfulness. But after time with His son Joshua, I picture God wearing a smile so big that it made His cheekbones sore.

To be a fly on the wall during their conversations would have been quite the experience. What questions did Joshua have for God, and in return, what promises did God share with Joshua? From my experience, when God begins speaking to you, it often revolves around who you are and what you're called to do. He establishes our identity as His children and begins to cast vision about the specific purposes He built us for. He uses passion to kickstart our hearts into coming alive.

This monumental moment is what I call *station identification.* Joshua had no control over his Hebrew nationality, being born into slavery, or his current season of wilderness wandering.

But the one thing he had the choice to do was be identified by God for purpose. He was positioned in such a way that he could ask God who he was and what he was built for.

This is arguably the most pivotal moment of every Christian's life. Here, not only does one gain an understanding of identity, but also of their destiny. Once you wrap your mind around God-given destiny, your direction is determined. Confidence is created when you know where you're headed, and even more so when you know that God Himself is going with you.

There is a popular saying that goes something like this: the two most important days of your life are the day you were born and the day you find out why.

This was the day Joshua found out why he was alive. Better yet, he didn't just stumble across an idea or think up a dream in his heart. The God of the Universe spoke purpose to him specifically. I think we all would take the opportunity for God to fill us in about our futures!

The fact is, that opportunity is available to you, as well. The Bible tells us we can approach God's throne boldly (Hebrews 4:16). What does that mean? We have accessibility to God and God has availability for us. We can establish our own Tent of Meeting where permission to linger has been granted. You can personally ask God what He thinks about you and what plans He's prepared for you.

You might be stuck in the middle of a mundane life or lack direction for your future. In the chaos of life, destiny lacks clarity. Still, God's presence is patiently waiting to speak to you about your personhood and purpose.

WE HAVE ACCESSIBILITY TO GOD AND GOD HAS AVAILABILITY FOR US.

INVITATION TO LINGER

Because of his proximity to Moses, Joshua was positioned near the presence of God. I can't think of anything else that would give you a greater advantage in life. If anyone understands that, it would definitely be me. I didn't realize it as a child, but my relationship with my dad built an unshakable foundation for how God wanted to show up in my life.

I grew up in church. By that, I mean I was literally a pew baby. I'm not sure what your church experience was like, but I was raised in an atmosphere that was the apex of Pentecostal Holiness. That translated to a faith that was strict, rigid, and legalistic. Long story short, our household wasn't what you'd consider *normal* for me and my eleven older siblings. There were no video games or watching TV. On top of that, we couldn't play baseball, because in baseball you had to steal bases, and that was considered a sin. You get the idea! It felt like I was in church eight days a week.

That type of environment developed an unhealthy theology inside of me. I knew what God was against, but had no clue what He stood for. The only things I thought God said back then were: you can't, you ain't, and you shouldn't. As a kid, I never knew the positive, affirming voice of a Heavenly Father. However, I did know my earthly father, and he was my saving grace.

He was the pastor of our church, but somehow, my experience with him left a much different taste in my mouth than my experience at church. Being the youngest of four in the house with dad and mom, I was his buddy that did everything with him. On top of being a preacher, my dad was the handiest guy you'd ever meet. With eleven mouths to feed, he was always hustling to bring in extra income. He took me to work on cars, fix furnaces, and rewire houses. As a boy, working hand-in-hand with your father is a dream come true.

I grew to love my dad but hate church at the same time. As I got older, that separation continued to grow more and more. Naturally, more freedom came my way, and I didn't necessarily handle it very responsibly. I dated a ton of girls, went to a bunch of parties - you know, the normal high school stuff. But my dad never stopped loving me.

One day, dad was riding shotgun in an Audi 5000 he had just fixed up for me. The day before, a brand new Ice Cube album had dropped, and I waited in line at Walmart to snatch it. The track "It Was a Good Day," along with every curse word in the book, blasted through the car speakers as soon as I turned the key. You can imagine, rap music was definitely off-limits for a kid who wasn't even allowed to play baseball! You could see the discomfort on my dad's face as he looked out the window, but he never told me to turn the music off. That moment of acceptance, without shame and guilt, taught me more about who God was than the thousands of Sunday school classes I attended growing up. It also hooked me to my father.

After high school, I dove further into rebellion. At that time, there was so much going on in the hood: poverty, racial injustice, and getting pulled over by police officers simply because of the color of our skin. I'd watch my father get stopped and interrogated for no reason besides the fact that he was black. I was not only angry at society but also at the church, because they were doing very little to address these real-life issues.

In a crazy turn of events, the only place I felt I could vulnerably express myself was through the Nation of Islam - the Americanized branch of Islam. I was desperate for a leader to follow, and attached myself to Malcolm X. Quickly, I became a student of human rights activism. As a freshman in college at the University of Missouri-Columbia, posters of Malcolm and Martin Luther King Jr. hung on the cinder block wall of my dorm room. I'd wake up and stare at these guys every morning, and it was almost as if I was trying to pray to them. I felt my dad's religion was weak and these men actually stood for something real. Looking back, it's almost as if God was setting me up. There was an undeniable hunger inside of me that I just couldn't figure out how to satisfy.

The friends I made in college were big into smoking marijuana. Even though I wasn't much of a smoker, I was down to give it a try. However, if I was going to do it, I wanted to understand the religion behind it. That sparked my interest in Rastafari. I learned just enough to run away from the religion - and from smoking weed! Afterward, I dabbled in Transcendental Meditation and Humanism, and began to believe that I was my own god.

All of this experimentation exhausted me! Coincidentally, trying to be my own god showed me how deficient I really was. I thought to myself: *How can I be a god when I need so much help myself?*

For me, my freshman year of college was a season of searching. I was trying so hard to run from the God of my childhood, but nothing else seemed to be working. Regardless of how much I tried to convince myself otherwise, because of my relationship with my dad, it felt like Christianity still had me hooked. Ironically, I still prayed whenever I was stressed about an exam.

Eventually, I hit an apex of spiritual confusion where I was not sure where to turn next. That's when God revealed Himself to me in a way that was almost spooky.

On a cold, snowy night, I was reading through a geography book in my dorm room. Suddenly, the most bizarre event of my life occurred. It's hard to explain, but I promise you, it was like a TV screen popped up in place of the textbook. Vividly, like a scene out of a movie, I saw my best college friend, Dionté, shooting a guy.

Crazy, right?! My friend in the room next door, Shane, was smoking weed. I assumed that maybe I was getting a contact high through the vents. Later that night I crawled into bed and BOOM! Now Dionté murdered the same guy on a TV screen on my dorm room ceiling.

The vision seemed so real it completely freaked me out. But the scariest part came when I felt pressure from God to go talk to Dionté. It was in the middle of finals week and I hadn't spoken to him recently as we'd both been busy studying. I wanted to run and hide from what God was showing me, but I felt responsible.

I gave Dionté a ring, and when he answered there was straight suspicion and paranoia in his voice. It seemed necessary that I go to his dorm and talk to him face to face. When I got to his room, it was the epitome of weird. He had all of the windows open in the middle of winter, and there was an undeniable eeriness in the atmosphere. That was unlike Dionté; he was a member of the football team and always seemed cool, calm, and collected.

"Man," I looked intently at Dionté, "I've got to tell you something. God's been talking to me about you."

I had no clue what to say. I was an unbeliever who was hopping back and forth between Transcendental Meditation and worshiping at the mosque. The only time I talked to God was when I was desperate for good test results! But someway, somehow, I just spit all of it out. I explained the dream in precise detail, all the way down to who was involved and the location where he pulled the trigger.

Dionté broke down in tears. Evidently, someone back home had beat up his girlfriend. Dionté's guys were on the way to pick him up from campus, drive back home, and kill the dude who did it. We called Dionté's friends, told them to turn around, and decided to pray together. I barely knew how to converse with God, but began to prophesy over Dionté that night. We thanked God for the plan he had for Dionté's life, and for preserving his future. That night, we cried and sobbed together for hours as the presence of God filled the dorm room.

I walked away from the Dionté's room and had my first personal conversation with God in years. I simply said, "God, if you're real, be patient with me."

Before I left for college, my mom gifted me a leather-bound Bible with my name engraved on it. After that night at Dionté's, I dusted the cobwebs from it, and read it privately every single day. I rarely understood what I was reading or knew what to do with it. Unsure of how to better grasp its meaning, I started writing out Scripture word for word in a journal. It was the only time throughout my college days that I had actual peace. Outside of my time with God, there was a constant battle with feelings of insecurity and inadequacy. But during my time with God, there was unexplainable calmness and confidence.

One day, I stepped off the elevator and into the hallway of my dorm building. Out of nowhere, God spoke to me with great clarity. He said, "I'm going to let you feel the weight I've been keeping from you."

The distance from the elevator to my room was forty feet at the most. But I kid you not, it seemed like an endless journey. The pressures of my life felt like they were physically crushing me. I legitimately did not think I was going to make it to my room. I remember saying to God, "If I make it to that door and You take this weight off me, I'm going to follow You."

As soon as I touched the knob, the weight lifted. God's grace absorbed all of the pressure from me. I opened up the door and was greeted by my dorm mate who was a minister. Overwhelming emotion overcame me and I began sobbing, telling my friend about my need for Jesus. He called two of his buddies over who had been praying for me during their Bible study, and that night I gave my life to Christ.

Looking back, God had His hand on me the entire time. When I was messing around with other religions, He waited for me. He spoke to me about Dionté, one of the friends who meant the most to me. He protected me from pressure that I didn't even know was trying to crush me. His peace surrounded my mind as Scripture got deep inside of me. Students that I barely knew prayed for me. Honestly, it is all so overwhelming to even think about.

The God who I was running from redirected my route back to Him. There was nothing I did to earn it or deserve it. To put it simply, it's just who He is. Without even knowing it, I had my own lingering experience. It's the time when God started to teach me that He hadn't given up on me.

I'll never forget a phone call I received from a woman in the church named Lily Lewis; it was right after I was saved. She was an old school, spiritual powerhouse, who probably spent more time fasting than eating. She had been praying and fasting for my salvation for years and years. Once I finally gave my heart to God, she had a message for me.

"David," she said confidently through the phone. "Do you know what your name means?"

"No, ma'am," I replied.

"Well, it means beloved," she answered. "You're loved by God, David."

I don't know if there are many other words in life that have helped me as much as those ones. I knew that my dad loved me, but I wasn't aware that God loved me, as well. It changed everything about the way I approached life.

Lily Lewis was the perfect picture of the character of God. She never gave up on me. For years, she fought for me when I wasn't even fighting for myself. The same is true about your Heavenly Father. When you're not even looking for God, God is still looking for you. Why would He do that? Because He has great grit and determination when it comes to your destiny.

God spoke to Joshua in the Tent of Meeting. His voice became loud and clear to me on the campus of Mizzou. He loves you enough to invite you to linger. He wants to be with you! Through the acceptance of that invitation, God will begin to build your foundation.

WHEN YOU'RE NOT EVEN LOOKING FOR GOD, GOD IS STILL LOOKING FOR YOU.

POSITIONED FOR PURPOSE

God developed Joshua during the time they spent together in the Tent of Meeting. However, Joshua was also developed on the battlefield. Let's re-enter the narrative of Joshua's life by picking up at the first place he was ever mentioned in the Bible.

While the people of Israel were still at Rephidim, the warriors of Amalek attacked them. Moses commanded Joshua, "Choose some men to go out and fight the army of Amalek for us. Tomorrow, I will stand at the top of the hill, holding the staff of God in my hand."

So Joshua did what Moses had commanded and fought the army of Amalek. Meanwhile, Moses, Aaron, and Hur climbed to the top of a nearby hill. As long as Moses held up the staff in his hand, the Israelites had the advantage. But whenever he dropped his hand, the Amalekites gained the advantage. Moses' arms soon became so tired he could no longer hold them up. So Aaron and Hur found a stone for him to sit on. Then they stood on each side of Moses, holding up his hands. So his hands held steady until sunset. As a result, Joshua overwhelmed the army of Amalek in battle. (Exodus 17:8-13, NLT)

As the Israelites were still wandering their way toward the Promised Land, they were attacked by the violent nation of Amalek. At this point, Israel wasn't exactly in fighting condition. As slaves for the past 400 years, they were accustomed to being used and abused. They didn't have the training to be warriors.

Remember, Joshua was Moses' assistant. Moses, being an old man, was more of a spiritual leader than a tenacious army general. But that didn't change the fact that somebody needed to lead the troops. Out of necessity, Moses chose Joshua to gather soldiers and defend Israel in battle. What was so special about Joshua that he became the chosen one? It could have been talent, gifting, or leadership qualities, but there's no mention of those things in the Bible, so there's no way that we can be certain. There is one thing, however, we know for sure: Joshua was the closest to Moses in proximity. In other words, God divinely positioned Joshua for greatness.

That's how God operates, by the way. We can get so fixated on skillsets and educational credibility, that sometimes we forget what a spontaneous adventure God's plan for our lives can be. He has no problem throwing us into battle. Are we always ready? No way! But destiny will work the same way in our lives that it did for Joshua. God uses unexpected opportunities to expedite purpose.

Even when I was questioning my religion, I never stopped going to church with my dad. Truth be told, I didn't have much of an option. Parents will understand what I mean. If I was going to stay at his house and eat his food, then my butt was going to be glued to a pew on Sunday morning!

Once I gave my life to Jesus, everything changed. I no longer attended church because I had to, but rather because I wanted to. A hunger for God, but also for ministry, began to develop inside of me. For the first time in my life, I honored my dad enough to become his student. I would pay attention to his preaching, dissect his sermons, and ask him all sorts of questions.

That was the proudest my dad had ever been of me. You could see the glow on his face when I was by his side on Sunday mornings. One day, I asked him in what ways I could help the church most. He responded by saying, "Well, David, I'm getting old. Why don't you take that question to God and see how He leads you?"

That's exactly what I did, and God responded! Several elders in the church started to confirm that I had a gift of pastoral leadership. The church was gracious enough to give me opportunities. I taught Sunday school before services on Sunday, even though most of the people in the class had been reading the Bible forty to fifty years longer than me. But it was crucial to my journey because they gave me a safe space to grow.

Honestly, I never had a strong desire to preach. However, one Sunday my dad asked me to fill the pulpit because he wasn't feeling up to the task. That day I preached my first sermon ever. Looking back, I couldn't tell you the title or what Scriptures I used, but I do remember feeling amazing afterward. As soon as church ended, I ran to my dad and exclaimed, "Dad! I can't believe it, but I love preaching!"

Dad looked back at me with a supportive smile and said, "Yeah son. I think you've got something on you. Just never preach for two hours ever again!"

Preaching wasn't in my plans, but it was in God's purpose. That's why it's so important to pay attention to where you are positioned. God positions you next to the right people and in the right places to pull purpose out of you. For me, God placed me next to my dad in an old, rundown church in St. Louis. Joshua was put next to Moses, and when unexpected opportunity arose, he stepped into his calling to become a victorious army general. It isn't a result of your talent or ability so much as it is God's positioning of your life.

Where has God positioned you? Because whether you're aware of it or not, there's purpose all over you. God's presence is available, and His purpose is always synonymous with presence.

You are, what I like to call, *dripping with destiny.*

REFLECTION & APPLICATION

1. Have you ever lingered with God? If not, set aside some quiet time and try asking Him this question: God, who am I?

2. Are you aware of what God has been speaking to you about your purpose? Write it down and pray over it.

3. Where has God positioned you? And who has He positioned you near? How can you start to grow, develop, and serve where you're at right now?

THREE

THE DISRUPTIONS OF DESTINY

I wish the fulfillment of destiny was determined solely by God's positioning. If that were true, Joshua's path to purpose would have been much easier. Heck, even my journey to pastoral leadership would have been smooth sailing. But that's not how it worked for Joshua, and it's certainly not the way things played out for me. You should know that on the road to destiny you will always encounter *disruptions*.

My hunger for purpose was activated when I preached my first sermon. That one message solidified that God could use me, and I was desperate to be used. Because of that, my favorite times during my college years were when summer and winter break hit. For me, that meant putting away the books, driving home from Mizzou, and giving full attention to ministry.

At the age of nineteen, I came home as zealous as I could be. In my estimation, it was time to move mountains and declare battle against the Devil! The church was small and struggling, yet big faith was stirring inside my heart. However, over that six-week winter break, my dad kept calling off services. Now I know that he wasn't feeling well, but back then he'd say things like, "Well son, we have to get that heater fixed." I was frustrated, to say the least.

My friend invited me to Bible study at his church on a Wednesday night, which stirred up more subtle annoyance toward the complacency at my dad's church. Afterward, I was excited to share the new revelations God downloaded in me at Bible study with dad. Secretly, I was hoping they might stir up a little bit of passion inside of him.

We would always meet in dad's room with him sitting on the rocking chair and me on the edge of the bed. I've never been one to hide frustration well, so after exchanging some small talk, I dove in pretty bluntly: "Dad, what are we going to do about the church? We need to grow this thing!"

At that time, I knew absolutely nothing about church growth. My mind was clueless when it came to strategy, structure, or discipleship. Like your average church member, I had no clue how to grow the church but desperately wanted the church to grow. God's Good News needed to be heard by more people!

My dad responded, "David, I've got a plan."

Jackpot! Exactly what I wanted to hear. My ears perked up and body language completely shifted on the bed. "Cool," I said, "Tell me about it!"

My dad didn't match that same energy level. At this point in his life, he was moving slow and seemed particularly tired on this night. He assured me, "David, just be patient. We'll talk about it tomorrow."

At this point, my frustration turned to anger. As soon as my dad said he had a plan, I was prepared to work all night, running purely on Holy Spirit and Red Bull! My dad was the plan guy and I was the action guy. I desperately wanted to take action! Instead, I went to bed, antsy to talk more with dad the next day.

I know that the Bible warns of letting the sun go down while you're still angry (Ephesians 4:26), but I was so mad that I was still mad in the morning! In fact, I decided that I wanted to teach my dad a lesson by playing hard to get. I didn't go to his room to hear about the plan, I wanted him to come and find me to tell me about it.

My dad wasn't up and moving around that morning as usual. My brother, Cedric, began to grow impatient as he was counting on my dad to lend him some money - as we all did! But as it grew later and later into the morning, there was still no sign of my dad.

Finally, Cedric knocked on dad's door and was met with no response. He knocked again - nothing. When he jiggled the handle, we all started to get worried. The door was locked. We started to yell in an attempt to wake up our dad. Still nothing. The reality that something had gone terribly wrong settled deep within my being. Worry quickly turned to panic, and we kicked in the door, hoping everything was okay.

I rushed to his bedside and my absolute worst fear was confirmed to be true. Dad was dead.

So many soul-crushing emotions ran through my heart: confusion, regret, denial. There was nothing that could have adequately prepared me for this moment. A shockwave of irrationality swept over me and I jumped on top of my dad's lifeless body. Somewhere between a yell and prayer, I shouted, "Come back, come back!" I laid in my dad's bed, sobbing and shaking. He never came back. My hero was gone.

Days later, when reality settled in, God began to speak to me once again. The only thing He said was: "Remember the dream."

In the chaos of everything, I completely forgot about a prophetic dream I had before the morning of my dad's passing. That night, two angels appeared in my room - one positioned on the left side of my dad, and the other on his right. He was walking up a stairway that led to Heaven. At that time, I had no idea what it meant. God reminded me of it to comfort me when I needed it the absolute most. In the dream, my dad had the biggest grin you've ever seen across his face. That was his new reality: smiling in Heaven with Jesus. That dream helped me get through all of the madness.

My dad died in January and just one month later I turned twenty years old. The first few months of that year were filled with mourning, among other mixed emotions, as I attempted to heal. Little did I know that would be the year I was grafted into leadership. My dad's death was the very thing that catapulted me into my destiny.

As I spent time reflecting on dad's life, motivation to not let his legacy die started to fuel me. The loving relationship I shared with him was undoubtedly symbolic of the type of affectionate relationship God wants to have with His children. Deep down, I knew that my purpose would always be tied to my father. And while there was no way to fully prepare for leadership by the time dad passed away, my years of attachment to him had served as a divine setup. God had been grooming me for ministry all this time without me even knowing it.

In that season, my emotions were running so high that it was difficult to see clearly. The particulars of my purpose were still fuzzy. As soon as my dad's funeral ended, the narrative shifted and I entered into a time of testing.

The undeniable question became: *who is going to step up and lead the church?* Unfortunately, he "tryouts" lacked integrity. It was a time when anybody who thought they were somebody tried to make their move. Maybe I was naive, but I had no clue how many wolves existed in the church.

My dad had an assistant pastor, but in my honest opinion, he was trash. He thought he should be the lead dog, but others in the church thought it should be me. Everyone seemed to make a run at the pulpit to obtain the power they believed came with it. I'll never forget some of the things that were said to me. Some said, "You're way too young." Others were selfish, saying things like: "You should give the church to me," "I'm going to take it from you," and "God sovereignly spoke to me that I should be the pastor."

Remember, at the time I was a heartbroken young adult. But I learned very quickly that I needed to stop grieving. It simply wasn't an option. I had work to do, and it was too important to wait any longer. Joshua would eventually experience a similar type of moment when his spiritual father, Moses, passed away. Almost before the funeral ended, God told Joshua to get up and lead the Israelites into the Promised Land. My grieving period didn't last long at all because the urgency of God was running through my veins.

One of my dad's highest values was education. He'd tell me over and over again, "Finish school. Don't let anything stop you from getting your degree." So graduating from college was a nonnegotiable. Yet still, members from the board were pressing me to fill my dad's shoes. I made a commitment to preach on Sundays, but I wasn't sure if it was the right season to hold the title of pastor.

Every weekend, I drove two hours from the University of Missouri-Columbia to minister at the church. At this point in my life, I have traveled all over the country to preach the Gospel. But looking back, those Sundays are still the most insane travel schedule of my pastoral career! My alarm would go off at four in the morning every Sunday - I bet some of y'all reading this didn't even know that was a real time! I'd spend time looking over my sermon notes, praying, and putting on my best Sunday suit. By 6:00 a.m., I was on the highway headed back to St. Louis, where I'd pick up Lily Lewis on the way. We'd grab McDonald's, scarf down some hash browns, and be at Sunday school by nine o'clock sharp. After Sunday school, preaching, and pastoring some people in the congregation, I'd start my two-hour journey back to campus and arrive by four in the afternoon. It exhausts me just thinking about it!

Those drives resulted in a lot of time in the car to spend *mushy moments* with God. The extensive miles on the highway became like Tent of Meeting experiences for me. For months upon months, over and over again, He'd speak to me about my purpose: "You're the pastor. I chose you. Step into it."

Truthfully, they were uncommon meetings with unappealing offers attached to them. God was telling me - not asking me - to pastor a declining church, with a deficient budget, in a depleted city. Even though my flesh begged to run from these mushy moments, my spirit knew to linger. These types of encounters are so misconstrued in today's time. It's the choice to trust God when it's disconcerting that creates deep wells in the dry places of our spirituality.

Today, most people chase wells instead of digging them. When it comes to the presence of God, the deeper we dig, the more of His refreshment we experience. But getting to that experience is both exploratory and exhausting; delightful and painful; clarifying and confusing. Those moments in the car were an opportunity for me to push past discomfort as God downloaded His promise deep in the depths of my heart.

One Sunday that same year, I finally surrendered. I had finally experienced enough mushy moments to know exactly what God was asking me to do. I was greeted with the normal pleasantries when I arrived at the church. People were excited to hear the Word, but I had something different in mind. My speech was planned out, and I executed it perfectly: "A few months ago, you asked me to be your pastor. After much prayer, I sense that's what God is asking of me, too. I couldn't be more ecstatic about the future of our church! So if you still want me, I'd be honored to officially become your leader."

I'm not sure what I was expecting, but it most definitely was not what happened next. Twenty-four people came to worship that day. During my grand commission, twenty-two of them left for good. They couldn't even wait until the next week to at least try to spare my feelings. They just hopped up and peaced out the moment I made my announcement.

I decided to forego preaching that week. Mainly because there was hardly anybody left to preach to! As everyone made their way to the exit, I stopped one lady and asked her why she was leaving. She responded, "We just all determined that you're too young to lead us."

That season became my *identification station*. I was shocked, confused, and hurt. Disappointment visited me often, which turns to doubt when left unchecked. God, my mom, and a few old church members were the only ones that believed in my leadership. More and more, it was seeming like those who left might have been right about me. They were the majority after all. But I'm so thankful God continued to speak to me about my calling in that season. Have you ever wondered how to discern His voice? Here's a tip: God's voice speaks clarity while other voices scream confusion. And whether I liked it or not, He clearly and confidently confirmed that I was called.

Looking back, I would define that season of my life as disruptive for several reasons. My dad passing away disrupted my development and role as a son. God speaking to me about pastoring disrupted my college experience. A majority of the church leaving me disrupted my vision for that season.

My definition of a disruption is something that interrupts the plan of action and causes disorder. Disruptions are always unexpected, uninvited, but also inevitable. Everyone would accomplish destiny if disruptions didn't detour, discourage, and dismantle us. Disruptions will destroy the vision of how you pictured life unfolding. They are the archenemies of your regularly scheduled programming.

Maybe your disruptions are more subtle than mine. On the other hand, they may be more dramatic. The question we all must answer is: how do I prepare for the disruptions attached to my destiny?

DISRUPTIONS ARE ALWAYS UNEXPECTED, UNINVITED, BUT ALSO INEVITABLE.

DRAMATIC DISRUPTION

After about one-and-a-half years of following God through the wilderness, the time finally came to enter the Promised Land. However, there was one big problem. Entering the Promised Land wasn't as simple as claiming new territory; rather, it had to be conquered. There were nations of godless enemies in the land that would soon belong to the Israelites, and they weren't about to give up their fertile land without a fight. It's important to understand that God's blessings rarely come without battles.

Even so, the Israelites were positioned for victory. Their army was numerous, Joshua was a fierce general, and most importantly, God was leading the charge. In preparation for battle, Moses appointed twelve of his best leaders to explore the Promised Land and bring back a detailed scouting report. Their mission was to return with a report about the land, size of the opposing armies, and strength of their mightiest warriors. The goal was to gain a tactical advantage.

After forty days, the spies returned with good and bad news. They shared the good news first: the land was bountiful, it was flowing with milk and honey, and there was luscious fruit for days (Numbers 13:27). But the negatives seemed to outweigh the positives: the towns were fortified, the people were powerful, and some of them were even giants (Numbers 13:28).

What is it about fear that so easily crushes the human spirit? Instead of being compelled by faith, the Israelites became paralyzed by fear. As the report spread throughout their community, the exaggeration of their opposition grew larger and larger. In no time at all, it was determined they would be devoured upon entry into this land of giants (Numbers 13:32-33).

As the Israelites began to make plans to return to slavery, two men tried to stop the madness and inspire the troops. It appeared they were the only two people out of an entire nation that were still ready to go to battle.

Two of the men who had explored the land, Joshua son of Nun and Caleb son of Jephunneh, tore their clothing. They said to all the people of Israel, "The land we traveled through and explored is a wonderful land! And if the Lord is pleased with us, he will bring us safely into that land and give it to us. It is a rich land flowing with milk and honey. Do not rebel against the Lord, and don't be afraid of the people of the land. They are only helpless prey to us! They have no protection, but the Lord is with us! Don't be afraid of them!" (Numbers 14:6-9, NLT)

I don't know about you, but I'd like to think I would have rallied behind the faith of Joshua and Caleb - grabbing my weapon and shouting a battle cry. After all, God was bigger than any giant they'd go toe-to-toe with in battle. And sometimes, you need someone to stir up your faith to remember that. Unfortunately, that's not the way things played out. Rather, the army responded to their general's pre-game speech by wanting to stone him to death (Numbers 14:10).

They rallied together alright, but not for God's cause. Instead, they plotted to kill one of their strongest leaders. Evidently, people will go to great lengths to avoid facing their fears. They thought it was better to sacrifice Joshua's life than allow the entire nation to be put in jeopardy. And if Joshua's day wasn't already bad enough, it gets even worse when God spoke into the situation.

"But as surely as I live, and as surely as the earth is filled with the Lord's glory, not one of these people will ever enter the land. They have all seen my glorious presence and the miraculous signs I performed both in Egypt and in the wilderness, but again and again they have tested me by refusing to hear my voice. They will never even see the land I swore to give their ancestors. None of those who treated me with contempt will ever see it." (Numbers 14:21-23, NLT)

All of the sudden, Joshua finds himself in a predicament that was unexpected and uninvited. He faced a situation that would inevitably detour, discourage, and dismantle him. God had spoken to him in the Tent of Meeting about his purpose, but this was not the way he pictured it unfolding. He had led his army to victory before, but now they had turned their backs on him. Because of this, God had to hit pause on his regularly scheduled programming.

Joshua was traveling the path to destiny but was now faced with dramatic *disruption*.

THE DEVELOPMENT OF DISRUPTION

God is in the business of using deconstruction to develop us. If something is unhealthy, he will tear it down to its foundation to restructure it better and stronger. The Israelites were broken and God committed to rebuilding them. However, in order to go forward, they first had to go back. A longer and deeper process needed to take place before they were able to carry the weight of God's promises.

God often walks churches, businesses, and leaders through this process. When it was time for my dad's church to enter a new season, he tore us down to the studs. He also initiated this process with the Israelites when He prohibited them from the Promised Land. Before they could *go*, they needed to *grow*. And while God works this way with groups, He also works this way with individuals. Whenever God rebuilds His people for promise, He simultaneously rebuilds their leader for purpose.

When everybody at my dad's church left, it initiated an important season of growth for me. Likewise, when the Israelites turned on Joshua, it marked a vital moment in his personal life. This is important because it brings hope that disruptions are not all bad for our lives. God uses them to deconstruct us, so He can eventually reconstruct us. Using the story of Joshua and my own journey as examples, we can see three things God does for us during disruptions:

#1 - Build Confidence

In a matter of minutes, Joshua's identity as a leader completely shifted. Before this, all he knew was victory. His record as an army general was 1-0. Then, not only did his troops refuse to follow him into battle, but God disallowed him from going to battle. I'm positive that any confidence he had in his calling was deflated like a beach volleyball popped by a needle.

One of the reasons I relate so much with Joshua is because of the extreme violence that came up against each of our callings. On that Sunday when twenty-two of twenty-four church members walked out, the only assumption I could make is that I heard God wrong. That morning, I had a powerful moment driving to church in which God confirmed my call to pastor the church, and minutes later almost everybody left.

At the time, this type of disruption was unwelcome and felt like a sucker punch. However, there was a silver lining in the pain. The same goes for Joshua's situation. The identical invitation God gave to us in our disruptions is the same one I'll extend to you: Develop confidence in yourself that is attached to God's affirmation, not the crowd's confirmation.

We tend to run when our identity is threatened by the insecurity of our calling. However, God invites us to double down and allow the roots of our confidence to grow deeper in His love and calling.

#2 - Overcome Critics

People left me and it stung, but man, I really feel for Joshua. People not only turned their backs on him, but they also tried to kill him! The same people who previously celebrated him as a heroic general now believed he served them better dead.

God uses these moments to develop thick skin. This part of your development may be painful, but it's also crucial. Why? The journey to a significant calling always includes significant controversy and criticism. How do we overcome the sting of the critic? By listening to the only voice that really matters.

As the story goes on, you will see that God never stopped speaking to Joshua about His opinion of him. The same held true for me. When everybody else abandoned me, God was still available. The Bible defines God as "ever-present" (Psalm 46:1). When everybody else turns their backs on you, God will turn His face towards you!

#3 - Surrender Control

God is after your control. Ultimately, that's a really good thing! It's not until we give up control that God can take control. And trust me, you want God in control of every area within your life.

The difficulty is that not everything that is good feels good. Giving up control can make you feel vulnerable and scared; it seems counterintuitive. We've all been in a few tug-of-war matches with God over our control. Sometimes, when we have a hard time giving it up, God will take it.

As an inexperienced, twenty-year-old pastor, God became my only option. When Joshua lost his army and was prohibited from the Promised Land, God became his only option. Because of the way life unfolded, we no longer had the option to coerce our callings into existence.

I define surrender as giving up something to get something. In this way, surrender is the posture in which God desires us to live. He gives us a calling with the intention of us surrendering control of it back to Him. Disruptions have a way of helping us hand our futures over to God.

WHEN EVERYBODY ELSE TURNS THEIR BACKS ON YOU, GOD WILL TURN HIS FACE TOWARD YOU!

For me, giving control to God came by the avenue of asking questions. My dad was no longer there to provide answers, so I had to learn to ask my Heavenly Father instead. A lot of them were simple questions but also left me feeling very vulnerable. I'd say things like: Where do you want me to go? Will you be with me? How can I know? And thankfully, God was always eager to respond. It's through our questions that we learn we can trust God enough to surrender.

DECONSTRUCTION AND RECONSTRUCTION

For two years straight, I'd drive every home from college every Sunday to preach to two people. When we were really packed there would be three! Upon graduation, I had a decision to make: was I going to continue to do this? It was tough because I finished on the Dean's List and had received job offers from all over the country. Some businesses offered me salaries of $50,000 plus bonuses! As a poor black boy from East St. Louis, I never anticipated opportunities like that. But as lucrative as the offers were, I knew I was called back to the city.

I came back to the St. Louis area and officially stepped into bi-vocational pastoring. After some very intentional hard work, our attendance grew from two to seven. That was enough for me to confirm that I was called, which is crazy. I suppose I could have set the bar a little higher than that! God got me committed for cheap.

My mom went door-to-door in that season to connect with people, pray for them, and invite them to church - partially to grow the Kingdom and partially because she felt bad for me. One Sunday, a man named Robert Miller came to church because he'd received a track from my mom. He was an older, retired gentleman, who wasn't in the best shape. Because of a kidney transplant, he had a tube constantly pumping medicine to his arm. When he visited for the first time, Robert had a weighted question for me. "Reverend Hawkins," he said, "when I die, will I go to hell?"

I walked Robert through the Gospel and led him to surrender his life to Jesus that day. Afterward, he went on to become my first deacon and biggest supporter. Regardless of how many times I told him it wasn't necessary to call me Reverend, he did so anyway. Again and again, he'd say, "Reverend! If it wasn't for this church, I have no clue where I'd be!"

For seven years, we didn't grow past ten people, minus the occasional bump up to fifteen on Easter. During that time, Robert Miller was the only person who got saved. That story preserved my purpose; it was enough to keep me going.

Looking back, everything that happened to me was crucial to pulling destiny out of me. The death of my dad, the church abandoning me, and seven years of stagnation all developed me. As God was building the foundation of the church, he was deconstructing and reconstructing me, as well. I needed the entirety of that time to find the strength to step out of the shadow of my dad. During year seven, God asked me clearly, "When are you going to follow what I called you to do?"

The moment I dismissed the vestiges of our church tradition was the day God started to grow us. The church went from seven people to fifteen, fifteen to thirty-five, thirty-five to fifty. That felt like an explosion to me! I was happy with seven and Robert Miller as my only deacon. But it was the beginning of my call to lead in an apostolic way. I learned about new foundations, structure, and strategy from articles, books, and conferences. I finally stepped into who God called me to be.

The disruptions deconstructed and reconstructed me.

The disruptions of your life don't have to end in damage. God's grace will weave them together in a way that develops you into who He's called you to be. He wants to remove the things that are hindering you and replace them with tools that will help you. His hand is still on your story.

Disruptions only destroy destiny if you allow them to.

REFLECTION & APPLICATION

1. What disruptions have you faced in your life? Did they make you bitter or better?

2. What current things in your life might God be trying to deconstruct in order to reconstruct you differently? They could be unhealthy habits, toxic thinking, self-reliance, or negative relationships.

3. Which of the following areas is God inviting you to develop right now: building confidence, overcoming critics, or surrendering control? How so?

FOUR

THE DIPS OF DESTINY

Let's recap the journey of our friend, Joshua. The man who was once dripping with destiny found himself in a place of disorientation and despondency. Why? He experienced a disruption - and not a small one either. It was a lifequake of epic proportion. Once upon a time, he was the beloved army general of Israel who was about to lead his troops into God's Promised Land. But suddenly, because of the Israelites' lack of faith, God placed a pause on their admittance. Not only did Joshua have to pay the price for the mistakes of his people, but they also blamed him for something he didn't do. And to the point of wanting to kill him! Talk about a bad day.

However, there is a silver lining in the story. Joshua, and his buddy Caleb, were the only men who had enough faith to stand up to the Israelites' irrational fears. They proposed that, although the battles before them were intimidating, they should still press on toward the Promised Land. And, while God was understandably upset with His people as a whole, He did recognize and honor the boldness of His two faithful servants. Here's what God said when He rebuked the Israelites:

> *"You will all drop dead in this wilderness! Because you complained against me, every one of you who is twenty years old or older and was included in the registration will die. You will not enter and occupy the land I swore to give you. The only exceptions will be Caleb son of Jephunneh and Joshua son of Nun.*

> *"You said your children would be carried off as plunder. Well, I will bring them safely into the land, and they will enjoy what you have despised. But as for you, you will drop dead in this wilderness. And your children will be like shepherds, wandering in the wilderness for forty years. In this way, they will pay for your faithlessness, until the last of you lies dead in the wilderness.*

> *"Because your men explored the land for forty days, you must*

wander in the wilderness for forty years - a year for each day,
suffering the consequences of your sins." (Numbers 14:29-34, NLT)

Put yourself in Joshua's position for a second. I'm sure there is a whirlwind of emotion running through your body. On one hand, you feel betrayed because the people you love dearly just rebelled against your leadership and finished a discussion about killing you. On the other hand, the God of the Universe just acknowledged your faithfulness in front of an entire community. You are the cream of the crop in His eyes.

In the middle of this tension, Joshua had to face an extremely disturbing fact. It was the most challenging obstacle that he'd been up against so far, in my opinion. His purpose of leading Israel into the Promised Land and kicking the butts of all God's enemies was still intact. But now, Joshua had to wait - and not just for a few days, weeks, or even months. His destiny was delayed by forty years.

Process that! Forty years is a heck of a long time. In our society today, some of us are ready to wage war when we get set back by forty minutes. Think about the frustration of a delayed flight, a traffic jam, or a friend showing up late to a hangout. That's the kind of stuff that seriously gets under our skin.

Unfortunately for Joshua, his delay was much more significant. It wasn't a minor inconvenience, it was a large majority of his life. We're talking about forty years that he can never get back. On top of that, it's not like wandering around aimlessly was something he wanted to do. The wilderness was a sucky place where food and water were not readily available. It was a hot, dry climate that caused agitation levels to run high.

To Joshua, it probably felt like an extremely prolonged prison sentence. And even though there was plenty of desert to explore during this imprisonment, it might have seemed more like solitary confinement than anything else. As an army general, he was wired to take new territory. The gravitational pull toward battle was in his blood. Not many things are worse than delays to a man with that kind of determination. While the Israelites wandered in the wilderness for forty years, Joshua's mind undoubtedly did as well.

What went wrong? Maybe I was a terrible leader. Will we ever get to enter this land? Actually, I am a terrible leader. What's going to be different next time around? God should pick somebody else.

Joshua went from experiencing a disruption to what I call a *dip*. What is it? A dip is what happens when enough disruptions accumulate in your life to throw it into a downward spiral. As you travel down further and further, there's no way to know when the journey will end and the pain will cease. A dip is often the root of darkness and depression in one's life.

Joshua faced the same inevitable tension we all do as we learn to follow God: He works slower than we like. Seriously, have you ever noticed that sometimes He moves at a snail's pace?! Problematically, human beings don't do well with slow, especially when it comes to our destiny.

I'll be brutally honest with you: you'll likely have an even harder time processing slow than Joshua. We live in a microwaved generation. We don't cook purpose thoroughly because we would rather have it quickly. Process is a completely foreign concept to us because we've grown accustomed to having everything - information, connection, and purchasing - at our fingertips the moment we want it.

When we look through the pages of the Bible, we see a pattern in the way God brings about purpose. He typically *bookends* us. This means that very shortly after introducing Himself to us, God often begins to speak to us about our potential. He casts a vision for what our purpose will look like as a final product. But there's always a middle ground that exists between potential and purpose. That middle ground is often where we find ourselves.

Another definition of a dip is the middle ground between potential and purpose. It's the season in which we must learn to do slow. Let me be completely honest: it's here that it can feel as if

God has tricked you. There was a time when He whispered sweet nothings into your ear about His plans for your life. But now, in the middle of the process, His plans seem very far from coming to pass. In the dip, the process of God is extremely difficult to discern, and the way He works almost seems disturbing.

It's not, of course. We see story after story in the Bible with God bookending His most beloved leaders and victoriously producing destiny through them - *eventually*. Think of Paul, who was absolutely legendary for the Kingdom of God. He planted countless numbers of churches and wrote over two-thirds of the New Testament. And before God ever spoke to him, He already knew the destiny that awaited him. But what did God do? He bookended Paul.

God prompted a believer named Ananias to pray with Paul, lead him to Jesus, and activate the anointing on his life. Before he engaged Paul, God gave Ananias a sneak peek into what Paul's life would look like: "But the Lord said, 'Go, for Saul is my chosen instrument to take my message to the Gentiles and to kings, as well as to the people of Israel. And I will show him how much he must suffer for my name's sake'" (Acts 9:15-16, NLT).

God basically said that the extent of Paul's significance would be proportionate to the extent of his suffering.

We love the part about significance, don't we?! We are suckers for all things success. But we hate the part about suffering. Yet, we see God tying those two things together in Paul and Joshua's lives. He will work the same way in ours. The extent of our destiny will be proportionate to the extent of our dip.

A.W. Tozer assigned poetic language to the dips of our lives. He said: "It is doubtful whether God can bless a man greatly until he has hurt him deeply."[2] In other words, if God is going to use you, He's also going to use dips along the way.

Dips may look different from person to person. Here are a few examples that might provide some clarity:

- Lingering depression that stems from the loss of a loved one.
- Unwelcome anxiety and panic that continuously show up when life gets stressful.
- The helplessness of watching your children repeatedly make choices that destroy their lives.
- Prolonged loneliness as you attend the weddings of friend after friend.
- Sickness that diminishes the quality of your life for years.
- Busting your butt at work just to be repeatedly overlooked and underpaid.
- Restlessness as the smallness of your purpose doesn't fulfill the vastness of your faith.

The picture I'm trying to paint is that dips always last longer than you'd like. So the question becomes, what should we do in the middle ground?

THE DEPTHS OF THE DIP

When my dad was taken away from me, I kind of assumed that was *the* trial I'd have to face in life. Nobody's life is perfect and everybody goes through something. Maybe it was wishful thinking or flat-out naivety, but after losing dad and a whole bunch of members from his church, I unconsciously believed I had hit my quota for troubles in life. Because of that, what happened next threw me into a deep, dark dip.

Shockingly enough, it hit me at the alter that I was marrying the wrong person. It wasn't because she was flawed or did something terribly wrong; instead, it went back to my upbringing. As a young pastor, I felt incredible pressure to get married in order to be viewed as legitimate. Church people often claimed they'd follow, honor, and serve my ministry *if* I had a spouse. And that pressure, plus my desire for marriage, created a cocktail of quick decisions. They led to my now ex-wife and I exchanging vows before we were ready.

Don't get me wrong, marriage is not only beautiful, but God also institutionalized it. But in the culture of my church, it had become an idol to some of the people following my leadership. And because I thought it was an answer to my influence issues, it became an idol to me as well. I felt as if I would always stick out like a blue elephant until I tied the knot with somebody.

My ex felt that same pressure. We were both twenty-five-years-old and had only been dating for one year. But because we were young and impressionable, we allowed the voices of pressure to replace the voice of God in our lives. It can be very easy to believe God is saying to do something convenient for you when it's something you really want. During our wedding ceremony, one thought kept creeping into my head: *you don't really know this woman.*

Although I was concerned, there was no going back. After our wedding, I was determined to try as hard as humanly possible to fix everything. Not yet understanding how to be a husband, I accepted it as my duty. But regardless of how hard we tried, things never got going in the right direction. Our core values were diametrically opposed to each other.

Instead of having a honeymoon, we had a hell-moon in Maui. My ex came down with an extreme case of honeymoonitis. What's that, you ask? To put it simply, she got cold feet. She had no desire to be romantic, and eventually, began throwing up continuously. We weren't sure what was up with her, so we took a trip to the emergency room.

After running a few tests, the doctor took me into the hallway to talk. The look on his face told me it was a conversation he wasn't looking forward to having. I grew concerned, thinking there was something severely wrong with my wife.

"Mr. Hawkins," he said, "I hate to break this news to you, but there's *nothing* wrong with your wife. She just doesn't want you. In fact, the fact that you're now officially married is making her physically ill."

Unbelievable! As a first-time newlywed, I had no frame of reference to process that information. For the next seven days, she stayed in the hotel room, most of the time not even leaving her bed. What was supposed to be the start of our beautiful journey together became a solo adventure. I explored the entire island by myself. I relaxed on the beach, went sightseeing, and even attended the famous college basketball tournament held there - the Maui Invitational. You can imagine that's not the way I envisioned experiencing Hawaii. But it was even more soul-crushing because it wasn't the way I anticipated the foundational days of our marriage unfolding.

The flight home provided a lot of reflection time. No brand new husband wants to sort out the thoughts of worry that ran rampant through my brain. I was in for a ride that I didn't know how to navigate.

Our marriage grew worse and worse, and it became obvious that it was built on a faulty foundation. Both of us put forth genuine effort, we just had no clue how to patch up the gigantic cracks. But we tried; boy did we ever try.

We built a house. We went on a dream vacation. Neither of those things made anything better. Looking back, it's so obvious that we were using life milestones in an attempt to medicate. Unsurprisingly, none of them worked, and in a final attempt to turn the corner, we decided to have children.

Four months into the pregnancy, we went to the hospital for a routine ultrasound. Just weeks before, the baby was kicking in her belly and everything was moving along just fine. However, the nurse didn't seem to be herself at this appointment. As she looked at the monitor, she turned pale white and ran out to get the doctor. The doctor looked at us with extreme concern and said, "You guys really need to go to the hospital right now. Your baby, Philip, is dead."

Just days earlier, we had painted Philip's nursery and put his crib together. The room was filled with toys and decorations that made it as special for him as possible. We even traded out my wife's car for an SUV. We were fully committed to this child. Furthermore, we were both secretly hoping that this newborn could repair the two of us and our broken marriage. Now, my wife was in a hospital bed giving birth to a lifeless baby. It hit us both like a ton of bricks.

While attempting to grieve from that traumatic experience, some hurtful things were said between us. On top of that, it was particularly hard for my wife to process how God could allow the death of a pastor's child. It really messed with her faith. Meanwhile, the only thing I knew to do was continue to preach. That hardened her heart against God, the church, and myself.

As we grew further apart, we continued to take drastic measures with the hope that they would bring us closer together. Through extensive medical testing, we discovered that our genetics would make it extremely difficult for us to have children. However, the doctors said we had a small shot if I got in vitro fertilization. I had a hard time processing the psychology that comes with that, but my wife wanted it, so I committed.

After two procedures and endless appointments, we tried to get pregnant again. To our surprise, it was a success! But it didn't last as we lost the second child as well. It was even more crushing to our spirits than losing Philip. We got our hopes up twice just for them to be obliterated both times. And it wasn't the only emotional trauma my wife experienced in that season. It seemed as if someone in her family passed away every month.

Everything around us was constantly dying. Our babies. Her family members. And our marriage would soon follow the same fate.

Still, we tried for kids one more time - I know, I know, it was a crazy idea. But looking back, I thank God that we did. If not, my son Josiah would have never been born. He was a miracle baby. He overcame every single statistic that was levied against him. Doctors only gave him a three-percent chance of living; and if he did live, the likelihood of him being healthy was a mere fraction of a percent.

Josiah's birth was such a joyful experience in our lives. However, as you can guess, it didn't fix our marriage. Nothing did. We went to counseling for over seven years. Somehow, that didn't even seem to make a dent. Even though we hoped a child would unite us, he ended up exposing our faults even more.

She grew more resentful toward me being a pastor. She felt that I couldn't lead the church and be committed to her at the same time. To make matters worse, it was in the season when we were experiencing what felt like revival to us. We had grown from seven to seventy and we were even moving into a new building. The tension in our home had become completely toxic and seemed nearly palpable. And now we had a child to worry about! The environment was too unhealthy for either of us to be good parents. That's when we finally acknowledged that our marriage probably wasn't going to make it.

We took every measure possible: a long season of prayer, an intensive counseling retreat, and conversations with godly men and women. Ultimately, we made the decision that we needed to divorce.

Although momentum had been building in that direction for a while, it was an extremely hard pill to swallow. As the decision to divorce became final, the revival in our church was escalating. God was doing something special. We had 480 people attending services and the community was being revitalized right before our eyes. However, in the meantime, I was busy fighting for part-time custody of my son.

I wasn't stupid. The reality that this separation would destroy my ministry was very apparent to me. In ministry, divorce is *the* kill shot that takes down pastors.

That season was the toughest of my life. Every minute of every day, I carried the weight of being a failure. I wanted nothing more than to carry on the legacy of my dad, but he had been married most of his life and pastored the same church the entire time, as well. Now here I was, on the verge of divorce and ruining what my dad worked so hard to build.

Those years of my life consisted of one disruption after another, which left me in a dark depression. My dad was gone. My babies were gone. The marriage was over. My career would likely end soon, too. All of this led me to the events that open chapter one of this book: when I was fumbling around with my firearm, contemplating suicide.

My fairy tale was hijacked. In my mind, there was no possible way that God could bring about any good from a dip like this.

FRAMEWORK OF GRACE

One of the greatest enemies of destiny is the faulty theology that teaches Christianity is convenient. That's why we have such a propensity toward dipping on God when life dips on us. Trust me, I understand that it's extremely difficult to stay locked in a dip. We feel as if it's prolonging our time in the waiting room of purpose. We grow unsettled and the urgency to get back on track tempts us to rush the process. However, each time we dip out of the dip we're in, we delay our destiny even longer.

In chapter three, we determined any disruption we face serves the purpose of developing us. A dip is no different. They develop us as well, just in a much deeper way. It's in the dip that we become desperately dependent on God. And trust me, that dependency is needed for where God wants to take you. You aren't strong enough to carry the weight of it on your own. The dependency you develop in the dip is the degree you need to graduate to the next level of your destiny.

There is a point in our pursuit of purpose in which God will mature us. Let's be honest - we really don't like that. We enjoyed the times when He coddled us, burped us, and changed our spiritual diapers. However, the infancy of a child only lasts a short season. Afterward, a good chunk of life revolves around growth. Our journey to destiny works quite similarly.

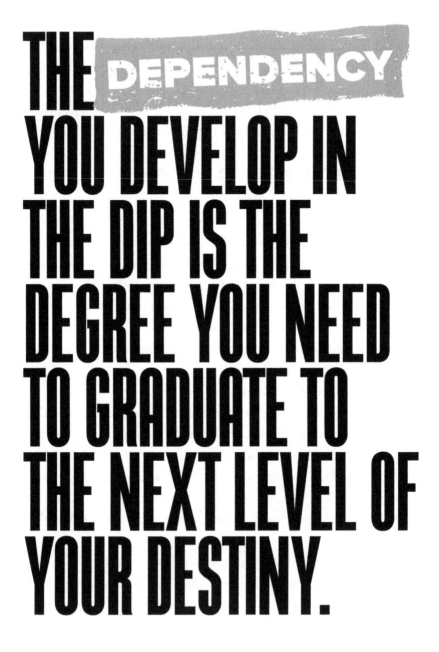

THE **DEPENDENCY** YOU DEVELOP IN THE DIP IS THE DEGREE YOU NEED TO GRADUATE TO THE NEXT LEVEL OF YOUR DESTINY.

Let's go back to Joshua. Using his life as a case study, we see a brief glimpse of success and then forty years of struggle. The Bible doesn't provide much insight into what those years looked like for him. However, we can assume that extended time in the dry desolation of the wilderness was fairly unpleasant.

It's in the dip that God purges you. You might think that sounds pretty intense. That's because it is. It's the time when He forms us to become more like Him. The next level He's inviting us into requires us to operate less like us and more like Him. He uses the dip to purge us of our selfish agendas, unhealthy habits, toxic thought patterns, and preconceived notions.

Because of our unwillingness to dive deeper into dips, we often misunderstand all kinds of Bible verses. A perfect example is one of Jesus' teachings: "But if you remain in me and my words remain in you, you may ask for anything you want, and it will be granted" (John 15:7, NLT). We think: *Awesome! God is my genie-in-a-bottle who will give me whatever I want.*

Sorry, that's not true! A better translation of the word *remain* is the word *abide*. To abide means sticking with God through hell and high water, and during that time, His will literally replaces yours. It's not about a wish list, it's about a transfer of wills. Here's what happens in the dip: God's will becomes your will. God's thoughts become your thoughts. God's ways become my ways. God's agenda becomes your agenda.

The dip creates such desperation that there's nobody else to cling to but God. In the case of Joshua, he didn't walk or talk the same way he did before he spent forty years wandering in the desert. His strength was gone and he could no longer use it to affect results. Instead, he became affected by God. The Heavenly Father imposed upon him to develop dependence inside of him. God is after the same type of dependence from you.

During my dip, God was doing a deep work inside of me. It was the most painful thing I'd ever experienced. However, there was a set of verses Paul wrote that helped preserve my mental health:

> *We think you ought to know, dear brothers and sisters, about the trouble we went through in the province of Asia. We were crushed and overwhelmed beyond our ability to endure, and we thought we would never live through it. In fact, we expected to die. But as a result, we stopped relying on ourselves and learned to rely only on God, who raises the dead. (2 Corinthians 1:8-10, NLT)*

Joshua knew ministry struggle; but Paul was the *king*. Throughout the New Testament, we follow his journey of missionary trips, planting churches, and bringing the Gospel to thousands. But simultaneous with the highlights was a whole lot of hardship. Paul was thrown in jail, beaten, and left for dead on multiple occasions.

We tend to read about Paul's story and overpass the reality of the struggle. We brush it off because we view him as a spiritual giant - and he was! But he was still only human. He put his pants on the same way that we do. He talked about how emotionally taxing his dips were - to the point of being too overwhelmed to endure. But when Paul could no longer go on, he discovered God's full repertoire of grace. Where our ability stops is where God's ability starts.

This concept is what I like to call the *framework of grace*. It provides an example of the extent of the parameters of God's grace. A few verses earlier, Paul explained why he was going through so much hardship. On top of that, he laid out the reason why so much grace was ultimately necessary: "For the more we suffer for Christ, the more God will shower us with his comfort through Christ. Even when we are weighed down with troubles, it is for your comfort and salvation" (2 Corinthians 1:5-6, NLT).

Paul endured hell. Why? Because the hell we walk through opens Heaven for those around us. In other words, Paul's dip wasn't a result of anything he had done incorrectly. God didn't unleash His wrath on Paul because He was angry. Instead, God used Paul's struggles to bring salvation to others.

THE HELL WE WALK THROUGH OPENS HEAVEN FOR THOSE AROUND US.

When I was sorting through my darkest moments, depressed and suicidal, that changed my theology. So many of us have adopted the narrative that says if we're perfect our lives will be perfect, but when we mess up, God will mess up our lives. When you break that ideology down, it shakes out to be works salvation. Because of this belief, the pressure of our destinies rests solely on our shoulders. It teaches the church that we need grace to be saved, but after that, everything else is pretty much on us.

The truth is that we need grace in every single moment. Paul did everything right but required grace daily. Joshua was one of only two Israelites to keep his faith in God but still needed grace for his destiny. And if they needed it, how much more do we need it?

God's grace was powerful enough to pursue me, pick me up, and restore purpose in the depths of my dip. I promise that grace can do the same for you - regardless of the messiness of your situation in life. The framework of God's grace is far more radical than we can understand.

The point is this: you need grace! We try to avoid dependency and believe that it's more admirable to take on life by ourselves. But the whole goal of the dip is to create desperation for grace.

REFLECTION & APPLICATION

1. Have you faced any dips in your life? Have you invited God to speak into those seasons?

2. On a daily basis, do you rely more on yourself or God? If yourself, how can you posture your heart to become more desperate for Him?

3. On a scale of one to ten, how big do you think God's grace is? Have you allowed it to work in the messiest areas of your life?

FIVE

PROMISES & PROBLEMS

Let's pick up the remote and fast-forward through the forty years Joshua spent wandering in the wilderness. In those years, he became deeply developed and desperately dependent on God. The wishes he had for his life were removed and replaced with God's will. How do I know? Because he's still standing. No man suffers for forty years and continues to walk the painful path of destiny unless he has surrendered all selfishness to God. Joshua graduated from the school of disruptions and dips.

I don't know about you, but I think that merits more than a diploma. Heck, it calls for more than the simple fulfillment of his destiny. In my opinion, he deserves for entrance into the Promised Land to be smooth sailing at this point. And maybe once they claim the territory, God could set up Joshua with a nice three-bedroom, two-bathroom condo on the beach with the mortgage and HOA fees paid in full! Doesn't that seem like the least He should do?

Where we pick up in the story, Joshua and destiny are finally about to have their long-awaited encounter. After forty long years, God finally gave him the nod to lead the Israelites into the Promised Land. Moses, his beloved mentor, had passed away, and it was finally Joshua's time to shine. Sure, he was eighty-years-old by now, but better later than never. The stage was set for the comeback of the century. This was the type of story that Hollywood turns into movies to rake in millions. But unfortunately for Joshua, it was anything but smooth sailing.

"Now the gates of Jericho were tightly shut because the people were afraid of the Israelites. No one was allowed to go out or in. But the Lord said to Joshua, "I have given you Jericho, its king, and all its strong warriors" (Joshua 6:1-2, NLT).

Hold up! That doesn't sound like an easy path to Joshua's beach condo. To enter the Promised Land, Jericho was the first city they'd have to conquer. Considering that the town was "tightly shut," it wasn't going to be a cakewalk either. Sure, Jericho feared the Israelites - mostly because God was on their side - but they also weren't going to lay down and get rolled over. Remember those giants that scared the Israelites away forty years ago? Now God's people were about to face off with their giant kids.

Imagine being Joshua: you spent forty years sorting through mental, emotional, and spiritual pain in preparation for this moment. Maybe deep down you knew it wouldn't be easy, but after everything you'd been through, you secretly hoped that it would! As you walk toward the Promised Land and see the entrance on the horizon, you see the many obstacles that await: a huge city protected by towering walls and barricades, armed guards, and fierce warriors that are two feet taller than you. What's running through your head? If it's me, I'm thinking, here we go again.

It's easy to feel the queasiness that would have run through Joshua's body as his stomach turned in knots. He had already been through this - paying his dues and then some. There were so many reasons for him to be anxious and angry, but at the same time, this was his only option. God doesn't shrink the size of our enemies, he enlarges the size of our strength. Our job is to stay obedient to Him when in battle. So Joshua walks forward in obedience, although likely frustrated with every step.

If you still don't get why Joshua would be so frustrated, let's break down the Scripture a bit more. The situation Joshua faced at Jericho seemed ironic, like an identical representation of the past disruptions and dips he had faced. Nothing ever went as Joshua expected it would. And whenever there's a gap between reality and expectation, you're always left with frustration. Joshua's expectation was that he finally made it, but his reality said there was still work to be done. As usual, there were obstacles that challenged his obedience to God.

Joshua was a man who was fully surrendered to God's voice. He was walking in obedience and letting God lead the way. And let's not forget God made a promise to the army general by saying he had "given" him the city, its leader, and its people.

Perhaps it's just me, but I definitely have a different understanding of the word given than God does. When I think of giving, the image of Christmas pops into my head. If someone is giving me a gift, it requires no effort on my part. My responsibility entails showing up at your crib, tearing off the wrapping paper, and enjoying the contents. There are all sorts of things I don't have to do: go to the store, wait in line, spend my hard-earned cash, wrap the present, and stuff it underneath the tree. That all sounds like the responsibility of the giver.

But God's gift to Joshua seemed to come wrapped in a gigantic problem: massive walls surrounding a city of battle-ready giants. Archeologists have since excavated Jericho to study the ancient city. They found that the walls protecting the city were six-feet-wide and seventeen-feet-tall. There wide, high, and rock-solid walls between Joshua God's promise of Jericho. As much as we want ease, God often sets us on a path of what feels like insurmountable obstacles.

The point I'm trying to make is this: a promise from God is never exempt from problems. At this moment, Joshua learned the same tough lesson that we all must eventually. God rarely gives promises outside of problems, but instead, right in the middle of them. We don't like that! We prefer God's provision without the intricacies of God's plan. Purpose without pain. Grace without the grind.

We'd be much better off to realize that there are always obstacles between what God says and what we see. Those obstacles can create a kind of tension, or mental anxiety, in our lives. But they are also what make the fulfillment of His promises so special. Think about it:

- The blessing of childbirth means more after experiencing barrenness.
- Hard-earned promotion carries more pride than preferential advancement.
- Prayers answered over years are more appreciated than

those answered over days. Relationships that have overcome difficulty are stronger than ones with no adversity.

- Tested leadership offers more resiliency than pure talent.

There will always be problems attached to promises. To reach destiny, we must learn to manage the tension along the way.

A PROMISE FROM GOD IS NEVER EXEMPT FROM PROBLEMS.

NON-LINEAR NARRATIVES

As people, we generally hate conflict of all shapes and sizes. I've read all the books on how to navigate conflict and I'm even a big advocate for engaging it healthily. Still, I can't stand it! There's something natural inside of us that would much rather stay inside our bubbles where it's cozy and comfortable. When it comes to facing conflict - please, miss me with all that!

Unfortunately, our desire for comfort doesn't change the fact that conflict is inevitable. Therefore, my goal is to help you learn how to manage the tension between problems and purpose the best you possibly can. The best way I know to do that is by shifting perspective.

Looking again at Life is in the Transitions, Bruce Feiler says, "Our society tells us we should be basking in progress, but our experience tells us that we are beset by slip-ups."[1] Listen, your life is not all doom and gloom! In fact, the Bible says that God is able to accomplish more through us than we would think to ask (Ephesians 3:20). But to live healthily, we must realize that life will not be a continuous highlight reel. We have to unlearn the expectation of basking in progress and learn how to wrap our minds around the idea of slip-ups and setbacks.

In an article developed for The New York Times, Feiler references a study from a psychologist at Emory University named Marshall Duke.[2] The study says that every family exemplifies one of three narratives through their family history. They are described by different directional patterns: ascending, descending, and oscillating. It showed that children who grew up with an oscillating narrative in their family turned out to be more stable in their mental and emotional health. We'll talk about that more in a moment, but first, let's do an overview of all the narratives:

#1 - The Ascending Narrative

The ascending narrative teaches that life always moves up and to the right. It emphasizes continuous growth, progress, and never-ending achievement. An ideal story of the ascending narrative would be one of a family who started from the bottom, worked hard, and made it big. Also known as The American Dream 101! Our culture is addicted to this narrative. If you zoom out and get a wider view of society, you might find that most people are consumed by the lure of better jobs, more money, and impressive pedigrees.

My point is not to draw a line in the sand and determine if those things are right or wrong, but rather to acknowledge that never-ending ascension is unattainable. People who stand by the theology that their lives should always be getting better often end up overly ambitious and anxious. They spend their lives trying to grasp an unreachable reality.

#2 - The Descending Narrative

The descending narrative teaches that life moves down and to the right. Maybe some things start well, but they never finish well. The theology of this narrative says that even if you start with everything you'll end up with nothing. An example would be someone who got their master's degree and became the CEO of a Fortune 500 company just to lose it all because of an uncontrollable circumstance.

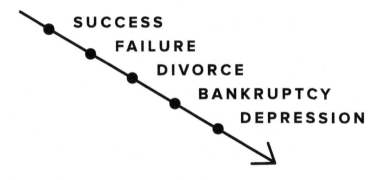

People who marry the descending narrative will likely be miserable all of their lives. While it's important to prepare for challenges, if you believe that life is only full of hardship, you'll quickly lose hope. There is no motivation to move forward without hope. Sadly, if you believe that the descending narrative is your destiny in life, it pretty much guarantees that is the narrative that will unfold in your life.

#3 - The Oscillating Narrative

The oscillating narrative is not consistently up or down, but a little bit all over the place. As you can see from the visual, it paints a picture that the outcomes of our lives are a bit ADD. It teaches that lives have ups and downs: destiny awaits, but disruptions and dips exist along the way. Joshua's story is the perfect example of the oscillating narrative. He experienced purpose and problems, hopefulness and hardship, obedience and obstacles.

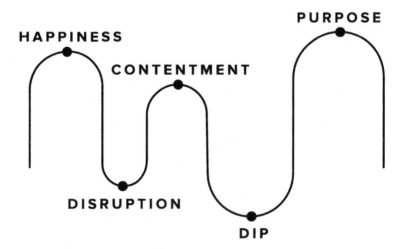

Children who are taught that life oscillates, and have observed the ups-and-downs of their family history, are typically best equipped to face life. One of the most important factors in the development of a child's perspective is their understanding that their parents are committed to them when life is all over the place. They grow up to be adults who better navigate the inevitable realities of disruptions and dips. Furthermore, they're not as likely to allow those events to deter them from their destinies.

If we're being honest, we all have certain life goals we are trying to achieve: graduating college, starting a career, making money, getting married, having kids, and hopefully retiring one day. However, it's not realistic to put a timeline on life. God doesn't always send disruptions and dips, but when He does, He will use them to free us from the pressure of perfection and production.

The Bible says it like this: "And we know that God causes everything to work together for the good of those who love God and are called according to his purpose for them" (Romans 8:28, NLT). When we love God and genuinely pursue His purpose, we can rest knowing that He will bring order to all of the chaos. Sense will be made out of your dips and disruptions. When things aren't going according to our plan, He still has a plan to make it all good.

When we learn to manage the tension between God's purpose and life's many problems, we can not only start to regain our sanity but begin to reach our destiny.

HOLD ON!

Looking back on the parts of my story we've talked about so far, it's clear that my destiny has taken on an oscillating narrative:

- I grew up in a Christian home with a loving father.
- Serious questions about my faith led me to skepticism.
- I studied Islam and tried out all sorts of whacky religions.
- During college, God pursued me through dreams and visions.
- In Gillette Hall Room 203, I surrendered my life to Jesus.

- My dad took me on as a church intern.
- My dad passed away unexpectedly.
- Church members asked me to be the pastor; I said no.
- I changed my mind and said yes; the same church members left.
- Our church wouldn't grow.
- Through our ministry, Robert Miller came to Jesus.
- I got married, but it never went as anticipated.
- My wife and I got pregnant, just to lose the baby.
- We got pregnant again and lost the baby, again.
- We finally had a baby on our third pregnancy.
- Our marriage ended in divorce.
- I almost took my own life.

Is it just me, or does that all sound pretty bipolar? I mean, seriously, it seems as if my life has been an endless rollercoaster of twists, turns, dips, dunks, and loops. Looking back, I'm just thankful that I haven't been ejected from the ride!

The truth is that nobody through the course of humanity has experienced a purely ascending narrative. On the other hand, I promise you that if you surrender control to God, you definitely won't experience a purely descending narrative either. Your life will likely oscillate in the same way that Joshua and I have experienced.

Up to this point, I've shared a lot about the difficulty of destiny, which was an important starting place. But for those of you who have stuck with me, we are hitting a turning point. My life turned around. Joshua's life turned around. That's the point: life does turn around. Destiny can actually be reached.

One of my go-to verses in life is 1 Peter 5:10: "...so after you have suffered a little while, He will restore, support, and strengthen you, and He will place you on a firm foundation" (NLT). If I were you, I'd highlight the phrase a little while. Will you suffer? Absolutely. But for how long? A little while. The best advice I can give, especially to the person in the middle of a dip or disruption: hold on.

For the person battling anxiety and depression is to hold on! For the person dealing with the pain of loss - hold on! For the person who feels inadequate and unqualified - hold on! For the person who wants to give up on God - hold on! For the person struggling with suicidal thoughts - hold on!

Disruptions and dips don't last forever and they most certainly do not define you. Rehabilitation and renewal are on the way.

REFLECTION & APPLICATION

1. Are you more likely to run from problems or hold on to God's promises in the middle of them?

2. Growing up, were you taught that life has an ascending, descending, or oscillating narrative? What could you do now to bring healing and health to your perspective?

3. Are you currently in a season that's up and to the right, down and to the right, or a bit of both? Either way, pray for God's strength in the middle of it.

SIX

RENEWAL

Repetition is one of the most powerful tools on the tool belt. Let me prove it to you.

While this book is being written, the video game known as Fortnite is sweeping the nation. The game is basically a whole different digital reality within our actual reality. Players not only create their own worlds but defend them as well - all while linking up with gamers from around the globe. Literally, millions of middle-schoolers all over the world spend hours in front of their TV screens every day, completely consumed by the wide world of Fortnite.

My son, Josiah, is no different. He has a deep passion for the game. Unfortunately for parents, one of the primary ways to experience all that Fortnite has to offer is by spending lots of money. A whole new level of determination comes out of Josiah when he needs my hard-earned money to buy a battle pass.

"Dad, can I have the battle pass?"

"No."

"Come on, Dad, I need the battle pass."

"Son, I said no."

"Can I have the battle pass? Please, dad, give me the battle pass! I need the battle pass. All of my friends have the battle pass. Just this once, dad, buy me the battle pass!"

I know, I know - this is triggering deep levels of pain and stress for some of my fellow parents out there. I feel you! This type of conversation might make you want to pull your wig off and throw it out the window. My first reaction is always to make Josiah stand in timeout for eternity! But what happens every single time? Josiah ends up with my credit card. It might not be the best parenting, but it's the only way I can get him to leave me alone. Please don't judge me!

Here's the point: the repetition of my child's voice changes my mind. Have you ever noticed that repetition tends to have that type of effect on us?

For example, companies show the same commercials over and over again in an attempt to persuade your purchasing. The first time you see a Mercedes commercial, you might not even pay much attention to it. But by the thirty-seventh time, you're calling the local Benz dealership! Furthermore, a wife might not feel confident about the dress she picked out for date night. But if her husband compliments her enough, she'll walk into the restaurant feeling like a million bucks. Come on, husbands - I'm trying to give you an easy win here!

Repetition has been proven to assist in the changing of our minds. Kids, parents, spouses, and advertisers all know it. And if we recognize the effects of repetition, certainly God does even more. After all, He did design the way that our minds think, process, and change. In the same way, my son used the tool of repetition on me, God used it on His army general, Joshua.

RENEWAL VIA REPETITION

As God brought Joshua to the precipice of the Promised Land, he observed the problem that stood between his army and God's promise: the gigantic walls of Jericho. We have already established that nothing ever came easily for Joshua on his journey to destiny. He faced rejection, betrayal, delay, the desert, and now a heavily-fortified powerhouse of a city. But God spoke to his warrior as he looked at the task before him. Remember Joshua 6:2, when God said, "…I have given you Jericho, its king, and all its strong warriors."

I'm sure the reality of extreme stress settled in Joshua's mind at the sight of Jericho. The future of an entire nation rested on his shoulders. Maybe forty years ago it wouldn't have been such a big deal. But let's remember, Joshua is no longer the young, up-and-coming, undefeated warrior that he was then. He was now in his eighties and had not only taken some losses but had a whole lot of time to wallow in defeat. His body, mind, and heart had been battered and bruised. He had been humbled in the process but had also lost his edge.

That's why God's words to Joshua were so important. "I have given you Jericho" was not an informational statement to complete the historical details of the narrative. Here, we see the example of a father coaching and encouraging his son. God reminded Joshua who he was and what he was created to do: fight, conquer, and take the land that belonged to Israel. It's as if God was saying, "I know it's been a while, son, but you're still dripping with the destiny I placed inside of you from the time of conception."

We have examined Joshua's struggle, but remember, disruptions and dips do not cancel your destiny - as long as you don't allow them. There is a point during every disruption and dip that God will renew you.

What is renewal? One way that the dictionary defines it is "the process of beginning something again."[1] For the sake of our study on destiny, let's define it like this: to resume after a disruption or dip.

Joshua's purpose had been in purgatory for forty years. During that time, he had every opportunity to become discouraged and doubt his destiny. There was plenty of time for him to come to terms with the reality that he was washed up and should hang up his cleats. But while Joshua had probably grown to think his destiny was dead, God knew all along it was only paused. So when the time came, He reactivated the play button. How did he do it? By speaking, motivating, and coaching his son.

God's voice is always the thing that sparks our renewal. His way of resuming Joshua's destiny was by re-speaking the words Joshua thought were going to come to pass forty years earlier. I know what some of you might be thinking: *How do we know for sure Joshua needed renewal? Maybe he stayed positive, prepared, and purpose-driven the entire time.*

We must look to Scripture to support our hypothesis about Joshua. I've been preaching since I was nineteen-years-old, so it's possible that I look at the Bible in a slightly different way. As I study, my brain often searches for themes throughout a story, especially when it comes to the character of God. Why? If we can catch God saying or doing the same things repeatedly, it teaches us a lot about His nature.

Remember the importance of repetition? As you break down the dialogue between Joshua and God, you'll see that God repeats Himself quite often in their conversations. In fact, if your significant other repeated themselves as much as God did, they'd probably make you want to drive off of a cliff! But God's objective is never to annoy or sound like a broken record. If He's repetitive, there's certainly a good reason.

In the book of Joshua, chapters one through five are all about Israel's approach and preparation leading up to the Promised Land. So much of that preparation is God engaging their leader, Joshua, in dialogue. It's where we find God repeating Himself like the local radio station that continues to play the top hit again and again. But there's significance in what He says. It can be found in the common threads of their conversations.

> *"…the time has come for you to lead these people, the Israelites, across the Jordan River into the land I am giving them." (Joshua 1:2, NLT)*

> *"…Wherever you set foot, you will be on land I have given you…" (Joshua 1:3, NLT)*

> *"No one will be able to stand against you as long as you live. For I will be with you as I was with Moses. I will not fail you or abandon you." (Joshua 1:5, NLT)*

> *"Be strong and courageous, for you are the one who will lead these people to possess all the land I swore to their ancestors I would give them…" (Joshua 1:6, NLT)*

"Be strong and very courageous…" (Joshua 1:7, NLT)

"This is my command—be strong and courageous! Do not be afraid or discouraged. For the Lord your God is with you wherever you go." (Joshua 1:9, NLT)

"Today I will begin to make you a great leader in the eyes of all the Israelites. They will know that I am with you, just as I was with Moses." (Joshua 3:78, NLT)

Talk about repeating yourself. What were the general takeaways of the continual conversations God had with Joshua? I am giving you the land. I am with you. I will not fail you. Be strong and courageous.

God initiated a constant conversation about what Joshua needed to hear the most, which leads us to a great point. God repeats Himself in the areas that are most relevant to your identity and destiny. He will give you the most pep talks in your areas of greatest purpose.

Joshua needed to hear that the land was being given to him by God because he didn't believe he was capable of taking it. The fact that God assured Joshua that He was with him means that Joshua felt abandoned. God implored his army general that he wouldn't fail because Joshua felt like a failure. And finally, Joshua needed a reminder to be strong and courageous because he actually felt weak and afraid.

God's voice is a powerful thing. During creation, everything He spoke came into existence - and we're talking about the skies, the seas, and the human race. Furthermore, we see Jesus use just a couple of words to heal people of disease and raise them from the dead. Whenever God says the same thing multiple times, the power in those words multiplies. It's important that we recognize the weight of repetition.

Just as God spoke to Joshua, He also wants to speak to you. What are the things that He's saying to you over and over again?

Maybe He wants you to know that you're not abandoned and He loves and cares about you. Maybe He continues to remind you of your destiny through the dreams that He's put deep inside of your heart. Whatever it is, you can rest in the confidence of knowing that repeated words are relevant words that can alter your life. The kind of words that renew your destiny.

THE TRANSFORMATION OF THOUGHT

Now listen, God can speak life-altering words to us for years on end. But change only happens when we allow God's life-altering words to alter our thoughts. As a preacher, I've learned that my sermons don't change anybody when they show up distracted by their lunch reservations after service. God could manifest in such a way that signs, wonders, and miracles break out. But if someone is only *hearing*, and not really *listening* and *receiving*, the best part of their day will be Applebee's two-for-whatever deal.

God changes us by changing the way we think. It's what is often referred to as *revelation*. In Greek, it means an *unveiling* or *uncovering*.[2] God uncovers new things about His nature, His love for us, our identity, and our purpose. These unveilings help us to think differently. Once we think differently, we inevitably live differently. The Bible spells out this concept in the New Testament:

> *"Don't copy the behavior and customs of this world, but let God transform you into a new person by changing the way you think. Then you will learn to know God's will for you, which is good and pleasing and perfect" (Romans 12:2, NLT).*

Transformation is dependent upon the way you think. If we want to learn God's good, perfect, and pleasing will for our lives,

CHANGE ONLY HAPPENS WHEN WE ALLOW GOD'S LIFE-ALTERING WORDS TO ALTER OUR THOUGHTS.

we must allow Him to *change the way we think*. When that happens, we literally become a *new person*. We're no longer the one who's bruised and battered. Left to our own method, our disappointment and discouragement would define our future. We'd see everything through a lens of limitation because we were let down. But when God touches our minds, our lives become new.

If you operate with a perspective dominated by the past, you're still the old you. But if you're future-focused and destiny-driven, there's a good chance God has made you new.

One of my favorite things is when our lifestyles and behaviors reaffirm things that the Bible says. It literally happens all the time! During my research for this book, I came across an article about the way our thoughts affect our lives.[3] It supports and adds practicality to Paul's teaching about the transformed mind. I'll do my best to summarize it for you as we go along.

Imagine your thoughts are visitors who stop by your brain; they come and stay a while before they leave and make room for new ones. Some stick around for only a short bit, then disappear completely without any lasting impression on the mind. Other thoughts rent out sections of your brain indefinitely, and depending on whether they are positive or negative, they might overstay their welcome. The point is: the longer thoughts stay, the more likely they are to gain power and affect your behavior.

This wouldn't be such a big deal if we had full control over the entrance door to our minds. We'd simply open the door for positive thoughts and keep it closed for negative ones. Unfortunately, it's not that simple. Thoughts enter the subconscious part of your mind. That means we often aren't aware they are present until we feel the effects of them.

The subconscious mind naturally processes every word and thought that gets lodged inside of it as a description of a real situation. Unfortunately, it doesn't automatically differentiate between anxiety and reality. Furthermore, it actually strives to bring those thoughts to life for the person who is thinking them.

How does this all look in a practical sense? If you constantly tell yourself that God can't use you, then you won't allow yourself to be used. But if you're always declaring that God wants to use you, then you'll become more aware of the opportunities to be used.

This is where repetition comes into play: the words that are processed repeatedly by the mind gain more traction and momentum over time. In essence, whatever you hear and speak the most becomes what you think about the most. And whatever you think about the most, shapes your life the most. Sounds pretty similar to "let God transform you into a new person by changing the way you think."

How does God change the way we think? If thoughts enter the mind subconsciously, then we must overpower them by what we choose to think about consciously. What forms our conscious thoughts? Everything we consume: the television we watch, the music we listen to, the books we read, the words we speak, and the prayers we pray.

That's why God's repetitive voice in the middle of Joshua's situation was so powerful! He used repetition to change Joshua's mind. For the past forty years, Joshua had subconsciously allowed thoughts of discouragement into his brain. Instead of building up his destiny, those thoughts tore it down. Through repetition, God replaced all the thoughts in Joshua's head that said *I can't* with ones that said *God will*.

Come on - that has to be a word for somebody! If you ever want to defeat the unhealthiness of your subconscious thoughts, you must become relentlessly repetitive about thinking healthy conscious thoughts. How can you do that? By doing exactly what Joshua did: locate the voice of God.

When your mind says I can't, God's voice says *I will*.

What toxic things does your mind lie to you about? Maybe you believe that you can't change. Maybe you think that you can't get back up after you fall down in life. Maybe you believe that you can't make any friends, or are unable to succeed, or unqualified to step into your purpose. Truth be told, maybe you can't! But even when you can't, God *will*. However, we must intentionally fixate our thoughts on His affirmative voice to give Him access to do so.

WHEN YOUR MIND SAYS I CAN'T, GOD'S VOICE SAYS I WILL.

ENGRAVED

Right smack-dab in the middle of my divorce, I had an angry and colorful conversation with God.

Everything was falling apart and my assumption was that my career in ministry was over. Bitterness overwhelmed that season of my life because I had worked so hard to grow the church, and in the blink of an eye it was all going to be gone. On top of that, it felt like I ran a wrecking ball through my dad's legacy.

Still, for some strange reason, God kept speaking to me about things I didn't want to hear: the future, His promises, being a tool in His hands, and moving forward. Heck, He was even giving me a vision for the church! At this point, I couldn't fathom that God would preserve my destiny as a pastor, especially at the same church. The toxicity that had crept through the door into my subconscious mind was too powerful. It sidetracked my own actions when it came to planning my future.

But God was so gracious to download a Scripture inside of me during that season. It seemed like it was written specifically for my situation, and it came to life in the middle of my lowest moment. Through it, He affectionately coached me back to health and began to renew my destiny.

"Can a woman forget her nursing child, that she would have no compassion on the son of her womb? Even these may forget, yet I will not forget you. Behold, I have engraved you on the palms of my hands" (Isaiah 49:15-16, ESV).

God was speaking to His children, the Israelites. The way they had been living was the definition of crazy, and now they were sorting through some of the repercussions. And even still, God promised that He would not forget them. In the same way that a mother will never forget her kids, God will not forget His people.

God took the imagery a step further to make sure we understand the extent of His affection for us. He said that we are engraved on His palms. Imagine taking a Dremel tool and engraving your name on the floorboard of a house. Regardless of who steps on it or how much weathering it endures, it's not going away. It is absolutely, 100-percent permanent.

In the same way, God has engraved your name in the palms of His hands. Regardless of the mistakes you've made, the sins you've committed, or the situation you find yourself in, He *will not, shall not,* and *cannot* forget about you! Every time God looks down, He sees your name and is reminded of the affection He has for you. His mind is always focused on the destiny that is meant for your life.

During my divorce, God spoke that verse to me over and over and over and over again. To the point that it was almost annoying! But it was exactly what I needed to hear. He was replacing my thoughts of destruction with ones of destiny. Just as He did with Joshua, He picked me up from the ashes and renewed my identity.

The words God speaks to you may be quite different than what He spoke to me or Joshua. But I pray that you take the time to locate His voice and allow it to transform your mind. It's time to start thinking differently; your destiny is far from dead.

REFLECTION & APPLICATION

1. Do you tend to think more positively or negatively when it comes to your future?

2. What have you been telling yourself that you can't do? Pause and invite God to speak to you about that doubt.

3. What's one verse you can memorize and repeat every day to renew the way you think about your destiny? Pick one that specifically addresses one of your biggest areas of discouragement.

SEVEN

REHAB

Post-traumatic stress disorder is a mental health condition that's triggered by experiencing or witnessing a terrifying event. During the event, one might not even identify it as traumatic. But that doesn't stop symptoms from sneaking up and affecting one's thoughts, behaviors, and well-being for years to come. If you've been through something traumatic, you'll usually experience at least one or more of the following symptoms: intrusive memories, uncontrollable thoughts, terrifying nightmares, detachment, emotional numbness, hopelessness, and the avoidance of people, places, and activities that trigger memories of your painful past.[1]

Most people buy into the myth that only those who have been to war will experience PTSD. That's far from true. Events such as childhood abuse, sexual violence, physical assault, threats, accidents, and deep emotional pain can lead to trauma. Some of you that are reading this right now have some degree of PTSD, but because you've learned to function with it, you don't even recognize it.

When not dealt with, living under the weight of trauma can limit your confidence, alter your identity, and distort your destiny. Obviously, none of us want that. And I bet I know what you're wondering: *Hawkins, how do I keep that from happening?* I'm glad you asked! There's only one way to overcome post-traumatic stress disorder: look your past dead in the eye and face it!

For those of you who have experienced any form of PTSD - whether severe or seemingly inconsequential - your first reaction to facing the past is probably: no thank you! When we experience hard things, we do our best to avoid triggers that might cause the pain from those events to return. When just a voice, smell, or sound reminds us of past pain, the natural reaction is to run. It's the way our mind tries to protect us.

Listen, I'm *grown*. And by that, I mean I've got bills to pay and people who count on me. Heck, I even get to claim a dependent when I file my taxes! But growing up, my mama was tough. Don't get me wrong, she was loving. But us kids would be acting like fools sometimes and she did not have the personality type that would allow her children to run all over her. When we'd start acting up in the car, she'd shoot us a sharp look via the rearview mirror and say, "If y'all don't stop breathing, you're grounded!"

Obviously, her parenting became exaggerated because our behavior was so extreme. But it's safe to say that it worked. When she said that, there was no more punching my brothers, kicking the seat, or talking. We all froze immediately. Here's what's crazy: as a *grown man*, if she says something in a certain tone, I freeze up the same way I did as a boy. Some of y'all who had mama's like mine know exactly what I'm talking about!

This is obviously a light-hearted example. But a lot of you have people you avoid, situations that make you tense, opportunities you refuse to step into, and emotions you constantly suppress.

God can't stand to watch you operate as a shell of the person you should be. He's not okay with you remaining on the outskirts of your destiny just so you don't get hurt again. That's why He brought Joshua face-to-face with the pain of his past. God will often position us to heal backward before we can move forward. That was the case with Joshua, and we can learn from his experience.

SHUT UP & MARCH!

After many rounds of coaching Joshua, God finally shared the battle plans with him. God was uninterested in his men marching up to Jericho just for them to get their butts handed to them. Nope - God wanted to win! He gave very specific instructions to Joshua about how the Israelites should take Jericho.

*You and your fighting men should march around the town once
a day for six days. Seven priests will walk ahead of the Ark, each
carrying a ram's horn. On the seventh day you are to march around
the town seven times, with the priests blowing the horns. When you*

hear the priests give one long blast on the rams' horns, have all the people shout as loud as they can. Then the walls of the town will collapse, and the people can charge straight into the town. (Joshua 6:3-5, NLT)

Some of y'all just read those verses two or three times, not sure that you comprehended correctly the first time. Don't worry, you aren't the crazy one - God is! We're used to war strategy that revolves around overpowering or outsmarting the enemy. But our crazy God drew up a crazy plan! Let's break it down into steps:

- Day 1-6: March around the city once per day.
- Day 7: March around the city seven times.
- Blow some horns.
- Have everyone shout as loud as they can.
- Watch the walls fall down.
- Go kick some Jericho butt.

Anybody else not signing up to follow those instructions? I mean, if God wanted the Israelites to increase their daily steps on Fitbit, He should have just said something. It makes no sense! But sometimes God will instruct us to do impossible tasks. That way, when we succeed everybody will know that His ability worked through our inability. Obviously, marching around walls that were six feet wide and seventeen feet tall wouldn't make them fall down. That is unless God showed up.

To Joshua's credit, he didn't get hung up on the craziness of God's strategy. In fact, he stood boldly in front of his men and commanded them according to the instructions God had given him. However, we will see that in translating God's instructions, Joshua decided to add a few of his own:

"Do not shout; do not even talk,' Joshua commanded. 'Not a single word from any of you until I tell you to shout." (Joshua 6:10, NLT)

Joshua sounds a little bit like my mama! The only difference is that instead of saying don't breathe, he instructs his army not to talk. Before this, he was relaying God's commands to his men in the exact way God had recited them to him. But at the end, he adds his own rules, and they're a bit extreme. Why didn't he want anyone talking on their daily stroll around the town?!

To me, it's rather obvious that the entire situation was triggering Joshua's PTSD. How can you tell when someone is triggered? They start to act irrationally and put extreme measures in place to protect themselves. And that is exactly what Joshua did.

Let's take the emotional distress of Joshua's past into consideration. Up to this point in the story, what have been his two most painful experiences? One was the moment when "the whole community began to talk about stoning Joshua." It came when Joshua tried to lead his men into the Promised Land and they rebelled. Forty years had passed since then, but it was still fresh in Joshua's mind. That's what PTSD will do to a person.

Unfortunately, that disruption led to an extended dip: God punished the Israelites for their rebellion. He told them they "will not enter and occupy the land" that He had sworn to give them/

For the last forty years, Joshua had been wandering in the wilderness. Why? Because his people ran their stupid mouths! The last time they talked they came to the conclusion that they wanted to kill him! All that talking led to the delay of his destiny and personal despondency.

But why did Joshua add his own amendment to God's instructions? Wasn't God's battle plan more than sufficient to lead Israel to victory and Joshua to destiny? The God of the Universe thought it up, after all! But the plan didn't suffice Joshua's PTSD. So he looked at his men and said, "Y'all shut up! I don't want to hear one word from any of you."

Although this was a new generation, he feared that perhaps the apple didn't fall far from the tree. Maybe betrayal had been passed down from their parents, the ones who screwed him over the last time around.

To be fair, the attempt to conquer Jericho would inevitably stir up some extreme emotions inside any of us. War is not for the faint of heart. But for Joshua specifically, the entire thing was totally overstimulating. First, God gave him a strategy that reminded him of wandering around in the wilderness. Every step around the walls of Jericho brought back memories of his many steps in the desert. Every day that the walls didn't fall, it felt less and less likely they ever would. It all seemed aimless and unintentional. But on top of that, every day they walked, he had to worry about his army murmuring complaints and gossip against him. The last thing he wanted was for them to talk themselves into stoning him again.

Thankfully, everything was different this time around. God was ready to let the Israelites cash in on the promises that were made to them. Furthermore, He was going to do the supernatural work of making the walls collapse and leading His people to victory. The only thing He needed was Joshua's obedience. Joshua may have been tentative, scared, and even a little paranoid, but he continued to walk faithfully in step with God's commands.

God could have taken down Jericho any number of ways, but He chose to do it in a way that triggered Joshua to remember the past that he hadn't fully faced. God positioned him to heal backward before he could move forward.

This is representative of the way God directs us into destiny. He positions us to face trauma, emotions, and faulty belief systems. He flirts with a fine line between reminding us of the past but never holding us captive to it. He wants to show us that we can let things go and fully trust Him.

This moment in Joshua's life shows God's way of doing rehab. What is rehab? The dictionary defines it as "the process of helping someone lead a normal life again after they have been ill."[2] By bringing his past to the surface, God was inviting Joshua to deal with it so that he could finally move on from it. Every step Joshua took around the wall was a step further through the therapy session that God had laid out for Him.

The entire narrative shows us a ton about the values of God. Sometimes we view our Heavenly Father as a taskmaster who doesn't mind using and abusing us as long as we get His work done. In reality, that's quite opposite of who God is. Time and time again, we see Him display great patience in His purpose of getting the Israelites into the Promised Land. He could have torn the walls down on day one and accomplished a great work. But He was willing to wait because working on Joshua was equally important to the work of conquering Jericho.

We live in an extremely production-oriented society. That's why we are often so focused on finding purpose. And don't get me wrong, God cares about purpose, too. He has countless conversations in the Bible with His children about His plans for them. But it's not just because He cares deeply about the plan; He also cares deeply about them. God cares about purpose, but even more, He cares about people.

It's important to know that God cares about you. That releases the pressure of wanting to accomplish purpose as quickly as possible to earn God's approval. It also gives you a different lens through which to view and process the repetitive issues of your life. God wants to heal you.

GOD CARES ABOUT PURPOSE, BUT EVEN MORE, HE CARES ABOUT PEOPLE.

THERAPY

Thankfully, the church never ran me out after my divorce. Some people tried. Many members formed a mutiny and announced their departure from my leadership week by week. It was expected, but also still hurt. Some involved were close friends that I supported through their worst moments, and now they were abandoning me in mine. I was broken after the toxic marriage, two miscarriages, and divorce. The betrayal made it worse. I was still the pastor, but a severely damaged one at best.

Healing was a necessity. Even though it felt impossible at the time, God put the pieces of my physical, mental, and emotional health back together again. He restored me as a leader - not a perfect one but one who was whole. How? Through a close circle of friends and therapy.

When a pastor gets a divorce, there are always rumors and speculation that spreads in the church. That was inevitable. But in the middle of it, I had a choice to make: what voices would I listen to? Some voices tried to tear me down in that season but other voices helped to build me back up. My sense of self-worth did not need to be torn down any more than it already was, it needed built back up. The Bible says that life and death are in the power of the tongue (Proverbs 18:21). Because I wanted to keep fighting for my life, the size of my circle shrunk and I only listened to voices who fought for me, not against me.

My circle was crucial in that season, but the best decision I made was to sit on a couch and talk to a Christian therapist. Arguably, the largest cardinal sin of the church is that we promote faith and healing over therapy. Don't get me wrong, healing through faith is real, and sometimes God performs such an action instantly. However, sometimes He restores your faith and heals your inner-world through the process of therapy. In my situation, someone needed to bring language to my trauma. When you start to understand your pain, you can invite God to heal that specific area.

During therapy, there were a couple statements my therapist made that changed everything for me.

The first statement: "Children are shockingly resilient."

My biggest concern was that my son would be permanently damaged from the divorce. But even now, when I look at the smile on Josiah's face, I know that he's in an environment where he receives love from both parents without the complication of any toxicity between us. It's a reminder of how messy God's grace really is.

The second statement: "You're not crazy."

During my dip, I always tried to fix the trauma I was experiencing. As a pastor, it's easy to fall into the trap of maintaining appearances. It doesn't represent the authenticity and freedom God designed us for. Throughout my marriage, I created toxicity in an effort to preserve the perfect, pastoral image. Because I didn't fully trust God, all of that weight landed on my shoulders.

Therapy was tough. We spend so much time surpassing issues because we're scared. One of the major goals of therapy is to bring suppressed issues to the surface and deal with them. Is it just me, or does that sound a lot like the way that God worked in Joshua's life? The PTSD had to be dealt with before he was admitted to the Promised Land. God loved him too much to allow him to walk with an emotional limp for the rest of his life. Joshua deserved freedom.

God cared enough about me to use the gift of my therapist to lead me into freedom. Truthfully, I felt naked the entire time. Vulnerability was not a muscle I was used to exercising. But that's the whole point. Half of the reason my dip ran so deep was because of my unwillingness to be real. Just like Joshua, God invited me to heal by looking back before moving forward. He surfaced everything I had suppressed so I could square up against it.

I'm still not perfect. That's why I've never stopped scheduling appointments with my therapist. Every fiber of my being believes that God wants me to live and lead from a place of wholeness. I don't want my unwillingness to be the barrier that stands in the way. Even though I have further to go, God has brought me a long way already.

My biggest struggle was vulnerability. Now I'm writing an uncomfortably vulnerable book. How did I get here? When you lead from wholeness and not brokenness, it becomes about helping others instead of helping yourself. Broken leaders break people, but whole leaders heal people. Most of the time, it comes at the cost of your pride. The Bible explains it as follows:

So to keep me from becoming proud, I was given a thorn in my flesh, a messenger from Satan to torment me and keep me from becoming proud. Three different times I begged the Lord to take it away. Each time he said, "My grace is all you need. My power works best in weakness." So now I am glad to boast about my weaknesses, so that the power of Christ can work through me. (2 Corinthians 12:8-9, NLT)

BROKEN LEADERS BREAK PEOPLE, BUT WHOLE LEADERS HEAL PEOPLE.

Our frailty and vulnerability activate God's best work. We rarely like this because it never feel good, but it's the way God works throughout the narrative of Scripture. He called broken people, and through the process of purpose, surfaced their weakness so they would rely on His strength. He did it with Paul. He did it with Moses. He did it with Joshua. He did it with David. He did it with the twelve disciples. He did it with me. And He will also do it with you.

How do you need to heal? Give your weaknesses to God; His grace is sufficient for you!

REFLECTION & APPLICATION

1. Do you experience any of the following issues? Intrusive memories, uncontrollable thoughts, terrifying nightmares, detachment, emotional numbness, hopelessness, or the avoidance of people, places, and activities that trigger memories of your painful past.

2. Ask God to reveal the source of your trauma. Don't run from it; write it down so you can deal with it.

3. Ask God how you can heal from your past. It might be specific prayer, talking to a mentor, or going to a counselor. Pray for the strength to be obedient to His leadership!

EIGHT

KEEP MARCHING

Destiny requires determination in the face of discouragement.

I wish I could tell you otherwise, but after the divorce, there were more discouraging days than encouraging ones. When suppressed issues finally start coming to the surface of your life, it seems as if they sprint there in a race for your attention. God surfaces our issues in an attempt to heal us. But if we aren't careful, a season that was supposed to bring about healing can create shame that destroys our will to move forward. It's a time when all of your issues accumulate at once and create intense adversity. For me, it was multiple things: dealing with the failure of my marriage, the shame of being a single father, the obscurity of leading as a single pastor, the hurt of friends abandoning me, and the fear for the future of the church.

When adversity builds, discouragement is often attached. It's important to be aware of God's presence and identify His encouragement in these moments. That's what prevents discouragement from overwhelming us, crushing our spirits, and ultimately deterring us from our God-given destinies.

During the discouragement following my divorce, my athletic training kicked into full gear. I had played sports my entire life: basketball, tennis, and track. These experiences developed grit and determination deep inside of me. Furthermore, they molded me into an intensely competitive person. Unfortunately, natural-born competitors have gotten a bad rep in the church world. Sure, competitiveness can be manifested in unhealthy ways like comparison and severe impatience. But it can also be extremely helpful when facing inevitable adversity en route to your destiny.

The attacks that came my way from church members and friends were painful. Trust me, pastors are susceptible to be wounded just like any other human being. The same things that hurt everyone hurt us just as much. But after punches were thrown, I made the decision to take a long, hard look in the mirror.

I had this question about the people who were attacking me: *Had they ever walk in my shoes?* They were great people, loved by

God, and the whole nine-yards. But truthfully, none of them had the capability to carry my burden.

God has a unique way that He goes about building leaders. He always seems to do it in the womb of obscurity. He bakes them in the oven of excitement and experience. For most, when the excitement wears off, and their experiences become more brutal, they abort God's formation process. Only great leaders sit down and endure the baking when the heat gets turned up.

God doesn't microwave leaders; it takes Him years to mold them. He knows that they must be cured liked concrete to endure the adversity they'll face. Looking back, I'm thankful that God had baked my leadership and concretized my character. Because of the experiences He had already brought me through, I knew I could get this adversity, too. He had already fortified me.

There were a few truths that solidified my confidence in the leader God had built inside of me. First was Romans 11:29, which said, "God's gifts and God's call are under full warranty - never canceled, never rescinded" (MSG). In other words, His grace is irrevocable. We can run from our callings, abuse gifts, or make stupid choices. On top of that, we can get distracted by the Devil and the chatter of the church. But all of that doesn't change God's mind about our callings, and I was called.

Here's a revelation: people draft, but God calls. What do I mean? People love the first overall pick of the draft. The promise of talent gets them excited. But when the first pick doesn't immediately produce, they'll downgrade the person. But that's not how God works. What He called and gifted you to be, you still are, regardless of what people say.

The second truth I rested in was the fact that God is the master of the resurrection. He's patient when giving us second chances. And He doesn't just give second chances; He gives third chances, fourth chances, fifth chances, etc. When the Israelites kept screwing up, God declared to Moses that He was "slow to anger, abounding in love and faithfulness" (Exodus 33:6, NLT). When people want you to give up, God hasn't given up on you. Often, the breaking point in our lives is God's making point. It's when He solidifies and fortifies His leaders. Instead of throwing in the towel, here's a great question to ask in low moments: God, how will you redeem this and resurrect me?

When I asked God this question, He started to speak to me about how He built and trained me to handle this type of adversity. It developed a determination in the depths of my soul that wouldn't allow me to quit. I knew one thing: if I was going to die or the church was going to die, it wasn't going to be a result of me giving up. I pressed forward and God became the wind behind my sails.

After the dust settled, about thirty families had left the church. That was expected, but what happened next was completely unexpected. The church began to grow again following my divorce. For a while, our attendance had plateaued around 425 people. But once my life fell apart, some new faces started showing up. The attendance rapidly increased by more than 150 people.

Our team had no clue where these people were coming from - since I was a single man again, we thought it might have been a flock of single ladies! But that wasn't the case. Entire families - mom, dad, and kids - made our church their home. It was extremely ironic. My family structure had just collapsed, but others were giving me the opportunity to lead them anyway. It was something that only God could do!

One new family in particular, the Andrews, was extremely impactful to me. I fully believe that God sent them specifically to encourage me when I needed it the most. Keith, the husband, was a military man, and one of the most loyal people I've ever met. God used them to restore and rehabilitate me in so many ways.

Once they had attended the church for a few weeks, it became obvious they were planning to make it their new home. We met at the church office and I spilled the beans: "I just want you guys to know, I'm going through a divorce. I know that's not something you expected to hear. Since you just joined, I thought it was only fair to give you the opportunity to leave with no hard feelings."

They looked at each other and smiled, then responded with words that were medicine to my soul: "We could tell you were going through something and that's exactly why we're here. We aren't leaving, Pastor David. God sent us here to help you."

It was there in my office, in front of a couple I hardly knew, that I completely broke down. It was so simple, yet exactly what I needed. We all cried and hugged each other. It was undoubtedly a God-ordained moment.

A week later, I was praying to God about the finances of the church. The thirty members that we had lost were all faithful givers. A lot of the new attendees weren't giving yet as they were still finding their stride at the church. It made sense but it also had me stressed out! My phone rang that Sunday night. It was a random call from the Andrews.

"Pastor," they said, "We were praying for you and sensed there's a person you've been contemplating calling. You need to call them."

They were delivering a word of wisdom that came directly from God. In my desperate state, I was extremely hopeful that this was an answer to prayer.

I made the phone call to a lady who was a part of our church and left a voicemail. I received the most incredible news when the call was returned: "Pastor Hawkins, it's so amazing that you called me tonight because I'm literally taking care of the bills right now. I'm going to do something special because I want to be a blessing to you. I'm sending the church a check tonight."

That night she mailed a check for $75,000. That was all the evidence I needed to know God still had plans for me and the church. When I called Keith to tell him what had happened, my voice was filled with the exuberance of a teenage boy. Keith let me know that this was just the beginning and he wouldn't let me die.

When I was on the verge of death by discouragement, God sent encouragement. Being a soldier, Keith scooped me up from my wounded state on the spiritual battlefield. He took me back to base and helped stitch me up. The Andrews family infused more life into me and the church than they may ever understand.

Truthfully, in that season, I felt I had every reason to quit. Some would argue that I should have thrown in the towel - some people were even begging me to do it. But in the middle of adversity, because of the people God put in my life, it was almost as if I wasn't allowed.

There were many negative things in the middle of my discouragement. Doubt was in the middle of it. Stress was in the middle of it. Hate was in the middle of it. The Devil was in the middle of it. But do you know what else was in the middle of it? People who were abundantly generous and supportive in my time of need: the Andrews family. And if that wasn't enough, God Himself was in the middle of it. He lifted me up and gave me the encouragement I needed in that season.

When God is in the middle, destiny isn't dictated by discouragement.

IN THE MIDDLE

Joshua was far from a finished product when he marched his troops around the walls of Jericho. God was still bringing him through the process of renewal and rehabilitation. His therapy sessions weren't a thing of the past but a present contribution to his life. Joshua did not have it all figured out but he did do one thing perfectly: *he marched.*

Do y'all remember the whacky strategy that God gave him to conquer Jericho? March around the walls once a day for six days and then seven times on the seventh day. Then do some yelling and the walls will come down. It sounds psychotic, but to Joshua's credit, he was obedient.

We like to overcomplicate destiny but it can all be boiled down to this: when God says *march*, put one foot in front of the other and march. That takes zero talent, skill, or ability. However, it will take some faith, grit, and determination. I've found that the people who are used the most by God are those who aren't afraid to get some blisters on their feet. When the going gets tough, they just keep on marching. Joshua and his men exemplified this in their conquest of Jericho:

> *...the Ark of the Lord was carried around the town once that day, and then everyone returned to spend the night in the camp... On the second day they again marched around the town once and returned to the camp. They followed this pattern for six days. (Joshua 6:11, 14, NLT)*

Every day, Joshua woke the troops up early, led them into enemy territory, then marched around the walls of Jericho. Think about it. Day after day, they took a lap around the town, vulnerable to attack the entire time. And if it wasn't enough that their lives were in danger, their egos were as well. What do you think that Israel's opposition thought while they watched their adversaries take an elderly-looking mall walk around their town every day?!

It doesn't end there; it gets worse - boy, does it ever get worse! The entire time that the Israelites marched they saw no progress. From days one through six, not even a single crack showed up in the walls. They returned back to camp every day just to report that no action had sparked - not even a little bit of pregame trash talk between them and the opposition!

Have you ever felt like you've been walking around what God promised you just to see zero progress? Sometimes we pray, fast, and cry out to God just to see nothing happen in our finances, health, marriages, jobs, ministries, and other aspects of our lives. When no cracks appear in the wall of our situation, discouragement begins to creep its way into our minds. Often times, we think it's time for success but God is still staging the victory. People miss out on their destiny when they fail to differentiate between a season of success and a season of set-up.

So what do you when you're waiting on your miracle? Exactly what Joshua and the Israelites did: keep *marching*.

God gave you vision for a business but it isn't profitable yet - keep marching. God promised you a child but you but your spouse can't get pregnant - keep marching. You're battling a disease and haven't been healed - keep marching. When your destiny feels impossible to reach - keep marching!

God might give you some wild marching orders that lead you right into the face of adversity, but when He leads you there, you can have confidence that you're not marching alone. If it was up to the Israelites to make the walls collapse, they would have been marching their entire lives. That simply was not something they had the ability to do. In my situation, if the weight of leading the church fell entirely on my shoulders through my divorce, then the church would have collapsed. But that's not how it works. If God sends you somewhere, He always goes with you. Pay attention to how the Israelites marched around the walls:

> *After Joshua spoke to the people, the seven priests with the rams' horns started marching in the presence of the Lord, blowing the horns as they marched. And the Ark of the Lord's Covenant followed behind them. Some of the armed men marched in front of the priests with the horns and some behind the Ark, with the priests continually blowing the horns. (Joshua 6:8-9, NLT)*

When you read that through a modern lens, the verse doesn't appear to mean a whole lot. But when we understand Jewish culture, it shows how God leads us through adversity into destiny.

The Ark of the Covenant was a chest that God instructed the Israelites to build as a house for the stone tablets of the Ten

Commandments. The commandments represented God's covenant with Israel and the Ark was symbolic of God's presence among His people. The scripture says that some of the army marched in front of the Ark and some marched behind it. In other words, the entire time they marched, God's presence was smack-dab in the middle of their efforts.

When Joshua relayed the crazy strategy to take Jericho, God's presence was in the middle. When the Israelites felt vulnerable to enemy attack, God's presence was in the middle. When there seemed to be no progress the first six days, God's presence was in the middle.

Regardless of what hell you come up against and adversity you face: God adds Himself to your problem. When He doesn't take your problems away, He enters your problem with you.

Whatever you do, please do not interpret adversity as God's absence. Whenever conflict strikes, it puts us in a spiritually susceptible state. We often use the comfort of our situations as a gauge to tell us whether God is present or not. We think if things aren't going well then God must be gone. But you won't find that type of theological narrative in the Bible.

God is our refuge and strength, an ever-present help in trouble.
(Psalm 46:1, NIV)

"Be strong and courageous. Do not be afraid or terrified because of them, for the Lord your God goes with you; he will never leave you nor forsake you." (Deuteronomy 31:6, NIV)

Even when I walk through the darkest valley, I will not be afraid, for you are close beside me. Your rod and your staff protect and comfort me. (Psalm 23:4, NLT)

"If I ascend to heaven, you are there! If I make my bed in Sheol, you are there!" (Psalm 139:8, ESV)

Throughout the course of the Bible, we see a theme of God's involvement in our lives. He is present in the middle of problems. He does not use our conditions to comfort us. Instead, His presence is our comfort in the middle of any condition.

Remember when Shadrach, Meshach, and Abednego refused to worship a false idol and got thrown into a fiery furnace as punishment? God didn't remove the fire, He showed up in the fire with them. His presence in the flames prevented their destruction (Daniel 3). God isn't into subtraction of problems, but rather the addition of His presence.

God didn't just order the Israelites to march. He enlisted in their army and marched with them. Throughout the entire Bible, we see him take that same posture. In fact, the Gospel narrative is a perfect picture of Immanuel, or *God with us* (Matthew 1:23). He didn't just bark down orders down from Heaven to redeem the world. Through Jesus, God became a man and lived among us. And now, by the Holy Spirit living inside every believer, God is in the middle of every situation we face. Our awareness of that is what gives us the strength to keep marching.

GO BIGGER!

While God was restoring and rehabilitating my life, a crazy thought popped into my head. My competitive mentality carried some of the responsibility for its origins, but on top of that, God was stirring up my heart. No matter how many ways I attempted to redirect my mind, I couldn't stop thinking: *go bigger!*

Typically, when you're in restore and rebuild mode, it's a time to retreat. But I knew deep in my spirit that God was giving us a window of opportunity. Our leadership team decided to put on the biggest Easter event we ever had. We rented out the 180,000-square-foot Gateway Convention Center for our service. The people who knew what I'd been through thought I might be going crazy - and maybe I was! But God had downloaded unexplainable inner peace deep down in my heart.

Throughout the process, I let God know that I was putting Him to the test. If we failed and it was a mistake to rent out the Convention Center, then my plan was just to be ordinary like everybody else. But I sensed something different. That's why I dared God to do the impossible. If this worked, it was a sign that He was restoring me in a public way so that my brokenness would attract the wounded and lead to their wholeness.

The Devil chirped in my ear the entire time. You know what his voice sounds like. I'm sure he was talking the same trash to me that he often talks to you: *You're not good enough. It's too soon. You don't deserve this. People will think you're a hypocrite if you do this. You didn't hear from God.*

Here's what I've learned: you can't control the volume of the enemy's voice, but you can control the power it has over you. He hates that I'm telling you this, but he only starts talking loud when he gets scared. As long as you're sitting on the couch, wasting away your life by eating potato chips and watching Netflix, you aren't a threat to him. But when you start making moves to bring people to freedom, he'll make his best attempt to shut you down. That's when he slings the best lies at you.

How do you navigate these attacks? Use his voice to your advantage. Know that whatever he speaks to you, the opposite is true. The lies of his voice bring validity to the truth of God's voice. It confirms your identity as a gifted and deeply-loved heir of Christ. His lies can actually create a confidence in who God has called you to be.

Your destiny kicks the Devil's antics into overdrive. That's exactly what happened to me, and I'm thankful I had the discernment to not allow discouragement to take over. Through the nagging voices, I continued to pray and march forward.

Our goal was that 1,000 people would attend on Easter Sunday.

YOU CAN'T CONTROL THE VOLUME OF THE ENEMY'S VOICE, BUT YOU CAN CONTROL THE POWER IT HAS OVER YOU.

At that time, it would have been the highest number of people that our church had ever seen in attendance. And when we put God to the test, He showed up and showed out. We were the first church ever to fill up the Gateway Convention Center with 1,200 in attendance that weekend. Even more importantly, forty-five people accepted a relationship with Jesus and made Heaven their forever home. The altar call lasted longer than the rest of the service, as people were really hurting and needed prayer. It's one of my proudest moments in the history of our church to this day.

Not long after, we decided to host a marriage conference at our church. If the Devil had ever spoken to me about disqualification, that was a time when he screamed it directly in my ear drums. It took a lot of humility and restored identity to host a marriage conference as a divorced pastor. I decided it would be wise to avoid teaching any of the sessions, but I did bring a bunch of friends, my therapist, and other experts who could help us in this area. As I marched forward, I realized that God was capable of using my mistakes to help others.

Many of you have dreams that God has spoken directly to you. Dreams about businesses, non-profits, healthy families, and unique ways to impact the world. The unfortunate truth is that the dreams of many people never become realities. God doesn't disqualify people from destiny but sometimes they disqualify themselves. It's not necessarily because they've made mistakes - God's grace is big enough for that - but because they've allowed the discouragement of failure to define them.

Please, let me encourage you for a second. The difference between your dreams remaining hypothetical or becoming tangible is saying *no to discouragement* and *yes to determination*. Stir up the grit on the inside of you and keep marching - God is with you!

REFLECTION & APPLICATION

1. Have you ever given up on something too soon? What would you change if you had the opportunity to go back and try it again?

2. What practices could you put in place to raise your awareness of God in the middle of challenging circumstances? Maybe it's listening to worship music, making a prayer list, or thanking Him for all the times He came through in the past.

3. What's one thing God has spoken to you about your future that you're willing to be extremely gutsy, resilient, and determined for?

NINE

THE SECRET SAUCE

Every day, the Israelites marched around Jerhico; then they marched some more; then they marched even more. Finally, after six days, it was time to take the city. Up to this point, not one punch had been thrown and not a single arrow had been fired. God's instructions were simple and seemed to lack creativity: *just march!* But day seven was when everything changed.

On the seventh day, the Israelites were ordered to take seven laps around the city and then shout at the top of their lungs. Then God promised to shake the foundations of the earth and cause the walls of the city to come crashing down. After He did His thing, the Israelites would charge into the city and take it captive. Days one through six were about walking, but day seven was about winning. Where we pick up in the story, day seven had finally arrived.

On the seventh day the Israelites got up at dawn and marched around the town as they had done before. But this time they went around the town seven times. The seventh time around, as the priests sounded the long blast on their horns, Joshua commanded the people, "Shout! For the Lord has given you the town!"...When the people heard the sound of the rams' horns, they shouted as loud as they could. Suddenly, the walls of Jericho collapsed, and the Israelites charged straight into the town and captured it. (Joshua 6:15-16; 20, NLT)

The many lifequakes Joshua experienced had brought him to this point. All of the betrayal, wilderness wandering, PTSD, and delayed destiny. Disruptions and dips defined forty years of his life, and because of that, he attended numerous therapy sessions with God. But Joshua finally felt the earth shake and saw the walls collapse. As the debris settled, he likely inhaled massive amounts of dust as he took a deep sigh of relief. Against every odd, Joshua finally experienced destiny. God delivered on every single one His promises.

There's no denying that Joshua's story is one for the history books, which makes sense, considering an entire book of the Bible is named after him. Seriously, the script of his life could make millions at the box office! It has everything that we're looking for in a narrative: ups and downs, twists and turns, dreams, failures, boldness, brokenness, and redemptive victory. It's the type of story that leads to tears and tissues. Why? Because it's a story with sauce.

Hawkins - there you go again! What the heck are you talking about?

Throughout this book, I've been brutally and uncomfortably honest about my life. Since we're already here, there's no holding back now. Vulnerability is tough, and the next thing I'm about to share is no exception. Ever since God told me to share this part of my story, my only prayer has been that you would meet me with love and understanding. Here's the honest-to-God truth: I have cheated on Chick-Fil-A!

Yes, you read that correctly. I'm a two chicken kind of guy now. I still love Chick-Fil-A; nothing could ever change that. But I've also developed some strong feelings for Raising Cane's. They each have different attributes that have made me fall for them. My many years of experience and a very sophisticated palate tell me that the texture of Chick-Fil-A is second to none. But the sauce at Cane's just hits different! And I'm willing to buy an entire box of second-rate chicken just for the opportunity to completely smoother it in a superior sauce. The sauce makes the blandness of the product taste so much better!

God is not in the business of writing bland stories when it comes to our lives. Our narratives never seem to be neat and clean. He probably hates watching movies with predictable endings, because that's not the way He directed any of the scenes in the Bible. Time and time again, we see struggle and suspense; it's a book filled with endless cliffhangers! Why? God knows that problems add sauce to our stories.

Because God was the director of Joshua's story, it never stood a chance to simply be *simple*. No way! The walls weren't going to fall down after praying one prayer. The Israelites weren't going to be victorious after marching one measly lap around Jericho. Joshua was never going to travel a perfectly paved path to destiny. Inevitably, destiny would require God's people to walk by faith when nothing about God's instructions made sense. Joshua accumulated some scars and scrapes along the way, but fortunately, those scars and scrapes added sauce to his story.

But why do our stories need to be so saucy? For those of you who are wondering, there are a few reasons:

#1 - Your Strength is In Your Struggle

God has a way of using the backdrop of calamity to build character. It's very uncomfortable because character doesn't come easy. In fact, I've found that character and comfort often oppose each other. And God is not nearly as interested in your comfort as He is your character. That's why He will strip comfort away to develop you. Strong character is reserved for those who have uncomfortably endured calamity.

The Bible says it like this: "Dear brothers and sisters, when troubles of any kind come your way, consider it an opportunity for great joy. For you know that when your faith is tested, your endurance has a chance to grow. So let it grow, for when your endurance is fully developed, you will be perfect and complete, needing nothing" (James 1:2-4, NLT).

Is it just me or does James sound crazy? It doesn't seem natural to be joyful when we experience trouble. Trouble usually implies stress, hardship, emotional turmoil, and picking up the pieces of life. Why would anyone celebrate that with great joy? Because sometimes what doesn't feel good *to us* is actually what is best *for us*. Trouble tests our faith by forcing us to rise to the occasion. As we do, we develop into more complete followers of Jesus who discover that all of our needs are met through Him. Genuine struggle produces a stronger Christ-

GOD IS NOT NEARLY AS INTERESTED IN YOUR COMFORT AS HE IS YOUR CHARACTER.

like character in our lives.

Out of Joshua's struggle came gutsy strength. He led his men in a march around the walls of Jericho for seven days straight with the only hope of victory being a supernatural miracle. Talk about risk! The repercussions of failure weren't as simple as Joshua being embarrassed for wasting everyone's time. It was a very real possibility that all of his men would die at the hands of their enemies.

It's difficult for anyone to stare death straight in the eye and move forward in obedience to God. But Joshua was a man who knew struggle. It had been one of his closest companions for forty years. Because of that struggle, he developed a Christ-like character that was willing to lay down everything for the will of the Father. He had the type of humility it took to surrender everything.

It's so easy to become bitter in your struggle but God invites us to get better. Consider all of the ways strength is developed during struggle:

- Humility is downloaded as you depend on God.
- Motives are tested and purified.
- The muscle of resiliency is strengthened.
- Intimacy with God is increased.
- Prayer becomes a constant practice.
- Empathy for others is enhanced.
- Purpose is pruned and clarified.

Without trouble, there is no struggle. And without struggle, there is no strength. What breaks you down will make you better - if you allow it.

#2 - Others' Strength is In Your Struggle

Let's briefly hit the rewind button on Joshua's story. Before Israel ever marched around Jericho or the walls fell down, Joshua sent two spies to scope out the land. He kept it on the down-low, probably because the last time spies went out to scout it ended in a murder plot. It went much better this time around.

Once they infiltrated the walls of the city, the spies stopped at the house of a prostitute named Rahab. We don't know exactly why the spies chose Rahab's house as a place of refuge, possibly because it was conveniently built into the city wall and provided a quick escape. It could also be assumed that Rahab wouldn't ask many questions when two men randomly showed up at her place. Regardless of the reason, it turned out to be a God-ordained decision.

God will use the most unlikely of people for the most unlikely of purposes. Not only did Rahab provide the spies with useful information to conquer Jericho but she also protected them. When word reached the king that spies were in the town, he sent out an order for Rahab to rat them out. But Rahab wasn't having any of it. She hid the spies on her roof and played dumb in front of the king's officials. She helped them escape Jericho safely in exchange for her own safety. The Israelite spies gave their word to protect her family when they came back to conquer Jericho.

After the walls collapsed, Joshua gave specific instructions to destroy everything and everyone except for Rahab and her family. Despite her broken past, God honored the prostitute by giving her a place amongst His people. And if that wasn't enough, God took the entire thing a giant leap further.

The genealogy of Jesus is listed in the first chapter of Matthew. Basically, Matthew acknowledges the family responsible for bringing the Savior of the Universe into the world. It spells out every name - starting with Abraham, the father of many nations, and ending with Mary, the mother of Jesus. Now don't fib - I know most of you barely skim over the genealogies in the Bible, so just in case you skipped over this one, we see something extremely significant about one-third of the way through it.

Salmon was the father of Boaz (whose mother was Rahab)...
(Matthew 1:5, NLT)

Hold up! Rahab? Like Rahab, the prostitute, Rahab?! It's commonly believed among most scholars that the Rahab in Jesus' family line was the same woman who went out on a limb to protect Joshua's spies. If God could have chosen any family line to bring his Son into the world through, why did He pick one of a former prostitute? It perfectly represents His redemptive work! God didn't pick a perfect family line for Jesus, instead He chose a redeemed one. It added sauce to Jesus' narrative.

Wouldn't it be just like God to restore purpose in Rahab's life regardless of her past? The downfall of Jericho resulted in death for all of her fellow townspeople but worked out unbelievably well for her. God's repositioning of Rahab changed history and left a legacy, but think about the timeline of how the events unfolded. She only entered the narrative of the story because Joshua's destiny had become a rollercoaster of stomach-turning disruptions and dips. If he hadn't been delayed by forty years, Rahab wouldn't have been a part of the story. The most likely scenario: her parents would have died in the initial conquering of Jericho and she never would have been born. God's destiny for Rahab was dependent upon the delay of Joshua's.

Did Joshua enjoy the disruptions and dips? Absolutely not! Were they painful at the time? Absolutely yes! Would he go back and do them over again? Not a chance!

But that's how God, the omniscient narrator, does some of His best work. The timing of our lives often tears us apart because we think God is absent, but we don't see what He is doing behind the scenes. He's not only working on our destiny as individuals, but He's also weaving the details of His plans for us together with His purpose for those around us. That's why the strength of others often lies in our struggle. Their power is unlocked through our problems.

When talking about his ministry, Paul spells it out like this: "He comforts us in all our troubles so that we can comfort others. When they are troubled, we will be able to give them the same comfort God has given us" (1 Corinthians 1:4, NLT). One of the reasons that Paul was so effective was because he went ahead of those he would impact and took on their struggles. It's as if he was a soldier on the frontlines of battle: he endured all of the first hits and he was able to help those who took on the second round of fire. Because of his experience in war, he could lead others to the same grace he had already found.

In this current moment, you are inevitably fighting some kind of battle. Will you allow me to coach you up for a second? You aren't fighting only on behalf of yourself, but also on behalf of others. God will strengthen you and bring you to victory. When He does, your vulnerability and testimony will become the hope of others. Your current struggle will qualify you in the future to speak into the lives of those who are struggling. The fact that you know the struggle provides the necessary credibility.

Whatever you do, don't give up! The fight is bigger than you. One day, you'll look back and be grateful that you pressed on, but even more importantly, others will be glad that you did, too.

BLEEDING & SUCCEEDING

In the previous chapter, we talked about the growth our church experienced on Easter. God absolutely blew the roof off of my expectations when 1,200 people showed up and forty-five of them gave their lives to Jesus. That huge win became a catalyst for the growth of our church going forward. New families continued to come and exciting things continued to happen.

Truthfully, insecurity was a battle I fought throughout that entire season. But in the middle of the fight, what God was doing started to take shape. It became obvious that the battle wasn't just for me. It was for the victory of others throughout our city.

In this season, our church developed an identity. We created a vision statement for that moment: *Love God, Love Others, and Serve*. My struggle changed the way we approached messy people. It helped us concretize what it really means to love: not in a fake and conditional way, but authentically and unconditionally. As our church has evolved, our vision statement has also. We now say that we are a place where anyone can *Find Healing, Restart Your Fire, and Make a Difference*. Healing has become a foundation of who we are today because of our willingness to welcome hurting people in a season when I was hurting, as well.

Our church became a source of refuge for those who were on the run from shame. Because the pastor had a past, it became a safe place for other people who had one as well. Unfortunately, the church in general has an ugly stereotype of ostracizing those who've made serious mistakes. Some ministries only accept people who have already cleaned themselves up from their past experiences. But the grace we read about in the Bible has no such limitations. Jesus' ministry was extraordinarily messy because He got into people's messes with them.

I'd often preach about the way Jesus treated lepers during that time. In the New Testament, people with leprosy were completely isolated from society because of the contagious nature of their disease. They were often exiled to communities away from everyone else and forced to leave their families behind. If anyone ever came into close proximity of a leper, they had to shout out, "Unclean, unclean!" Everyone would avoid them like the plague.

Here's what's ironic: the people everyone ran away from because of their disease are the same people Jesus ran toward. There are several accounts of Jesus healing lepers in the Bible, and He even went as far as touching them despite their condition.

Our church became a place where lepers were welcome - the more, the merrier! Why? Because that meant we were doing something meaningful. We no longer had an interest in doing church for stuffy church people. We became a church for the broken, lost, and hurting.

CHURCH IS A PLACE TO CLOTHE SINFUL PEOPLE WITH GRACE, NOT EXPOSE THEIR SIN WITH SHAME.

As the leader, God allowed me to bleed but also succeed. People saw God's public restoration of me and it gave them the courage they needed to find healing. Many people were set free from the shame of their divorce, past addictions, and emotional trauma. People who thought they would never be used by God became leaders in the church. God gave them back their swag. The freedom that was activated almost felt physical and tangible.

One day in particular, a man who was close to leadership came to a meeting drunk. He had previously been an alcoholic and slipped up due to some demons he was facing. Inevitably, people started to panic and wanted to protect the image of the church. When they ran to me for guidance, I simply said, "Y'all better leave him here."

It was a teaching moment, but also a defining moment for the heart of our church. If someone had enough gumption to come to church in their brokenness, the least we can do is love them through their brokenness. Church is a place to clothe sinful people with grace, not expose their sin with shame. My own struggle allowed me to see this man through the eyes of Jesus. I was able to look past his sin and into the vulnerability of his humanity.

Make no mistake about it - my struggle sucked! But it not only became my strength, it also became the strength of others. Hundreds of lives were impacted on the other side. In the same way, your struggle is the secret sauce of your story. God will use what sucks to bring about the salvation of others.

REFLECTION & APPLICATION

1. What's your biggest struggle right now? How might God be using it to write your story?

2. How can you use the struggle you've been through to help other people?

3. When you come into close contact with someone who has issues, do you judge them or love them first? Continue to pray for the grace to see people as Jesus sees you.

TEN

DESTINY

It's important that we conclude by tackling the most important question of the entire book: what is destiny?

I know, I know - I've used the word about 572 times so far and waited until chapter ten to breakdown what it means. Don't worry, there is a reason for that. This book is not only an encouragement to help you through the disruptions and dips of life, but it's also a guide to your destiny. My prayer is that you'd use the lives of Joshua and myself as case studies to help you interpret and conquer the disruptions and dips that knock on your door. Even more than that, I want you to know that God has not directed the narrative of your life just so you could make it through the disruptions and dips. The end goal is always destiny! God brings clarity to the calamity of life through the following equation: disruptions + dips = destiny.

My observation as a pastor is that some who have been through disruptions and dips live the rest of their lives experiencing underlying discouragement or even depression. They never bounce back because they allow bitterness to consume their present state of affairs as well as their future. Why is that? In my opinion, it's because many have a skewed definition of destiny. Because they don't understand God's version of destiny, they're left searching for what they assumed it to be. Unfortunately, when you go on that type of search, you'll never find the satisfaction your soul craves.

The ills of 21st-century culture have infiltrated and infected Christianity's version of destiny. We live in a society that's completely consumed with fans, followers, likes, and going viral. We associate success with posting a picture in a Gucci belt or pulling up to a preaching engagement in a Tesla. We confuse building God's kingdom with building our own, being an influencer on social media with having real influence in someone's life, getting a heart on Instagram with someone surrendering their heart to Jesus.

When we expect that serving God will result in fame or accolades, our view of destiny becomes extremely distorted. What happens when we're left still wearing a belt from Kohl's and still driving an old Honda? When our experiences don't turn out to match our expectations, toxic thinking tells us we didn't get *what we deserved* or that *God didn't come through.*

God doesn't want you famous, He wants you faithful. That's why my working definition of destiny isn't rooted in cultural values or societal expectations. Instead, it's Biblically sourced and stems from personal experience. I believe that the healthiness found within it is enough to lead you - and also those around you - to freedom.

Destiny is the root word of destination. Therefore, destiny is a place that each moment of our lives is moving toward. But the destination isn't a vacation spot for our self-gratification; rather, it's one that requires our humility and surrender. It isn't a place of self-indulgence; it's one of self-sacrifice. Our arrival isn't just for our own good, but also for the good of others. We reach our destiny when we arrive at a place in our lives where we're able to authentically serve others in a way that genuinely helps them. It's using our position in life to help "the least of these" (Matthew 25:40, NLT), or those who haven't yet reached the place where we reside.

Some of you have bought into the lie that destiny implies bigger things in your life: *bigger* houses, *bigger* followings, and *bigger* paychecks. Don't get me wrong, God might bless you in big ways. But big is not the destination. Becoming *big* in God's Kingdom begins with your willingness to get *small.* It's what John the Baptist said about the shrinking of his ministry in comparison to the growth of Jesus' ministry: "'He must become greater and greater, and I must become less and less'" (John 3:30, NLT). Destiny isn't about maximizing ourselves; it's about our willingness to minimize ourselves to allow God to be the one who is maximized.

Through disruptions and dips, God purged me of all character traits that weren't necessary for my destiny. He humbled me in a way that helped me look less like myself and more like Him. He did the same thing to Joshua, and it produced amazing results.

BECOMING BIG IN GOD'S KINGDOM BEGINS WITH YOUR WILLINGNESS TO GET SMALL.

AS FOR ME & MY HOUSE

As we finally near the end of Joshua's story, we see a near-storybook ending. After everything he went through - disruptions, dips, discouragement, despondency, and any other d-words I might be forgetting - God finally rewards his persistent pursuit of destiny.

So the Lord was with Joshua, and his fame spread throughout the land. (Joshua 6:27, NIV)

After reading this book and observing the depths of Joshua's struggle, I hope this verse makes you happy for him. Throughout his life, he wrestled with the question: *Is God with me?* That's why God repeatedly reminded him that He was, indeed, with Joshua through his many disruptions and dips. This verse follows shortly after the walls of Jericho have collapsed and the Israelites have taken the city. God's presence in His cherished leader's life was no longer a question but rather a statement. It was written with a sense of finality: "the Lord was with Joshua."

That assurance was the only thing Joshua needed. At the end of the day, God's presence - not achievements or accolades - was the only thing that made Joshua healthy and whole. However, because Joshua was faithful to God through hell and high water, he did earn a lot of recognition - even fame - for it. Joshua didn't gain notoriety because he posted popular preach clips on TikTok or because Instagram verified him with the blue checkmark. He became famous because he gave his life for the good of others. Because of his endurance, he led not just himself but an entire nation to the promise of God. Joshua's fame wasn't about Joshua, it was about the God he served.

There are many different words that we use for fame: influence, notoriety, and popularity. Regardless of your term of choice, fame is an allusive idea that people will finally notice us and we'll finally be important. From a Biblical lens, real fame is when others take notice of your example because of the selflessness of your servanthood.

Fame is a funny thing. Anyone who wants fame should also be willing to endure a great deal of pain. People who pursue popularity without the expectation of hardship are in for a rude awakening. The Bible defines Joshua as famous but also describes his preceding difficulties in vivid detail. Recognition only came after betrayal, broken relationships, failure, and emotional distress. On the same note, my life is different today than it was during my divorce. For some reason, God has chosen me, a broken vessel, to build the church. But behind every story of success is a scar that most people never see.

For this reason, I'd like to propose that Joshua 6:27 isn't the best representation and reflection of Joshua's destiny. Fame is an important part of his story, sure, but it also wasn't what his life was all about. Joshua was never in pursuit of success, only servanthood. Purpose, not popularity, is what drove him to keep moving forward during his forty-year delay. Faithfulness, not fame, is the best word to describe his life.

So what is the verse we can use to accurately honor the man who gave everything he had for God-given destiny? Toward the end of his eponymous book, Joshua stood in front of Israel at 110-years-old. Knowing that death was near, the wise sage wanted to implore and challenge his people one final time. He began his speech by reflecting on everything God had brought them through: deliverance from slavery, forty years in the wilderness, the walls of Jericho, and numerous battles to fully inherit the Promised Land.

Joshua challenged his people to throw aside every idol as an act of faithfulness to God. The way that God had cared and fought for them was unprecedented, after all. In his final motivational speech to the Israelites, Joshua asked them to draw a line in the sand and determine who they would serve. To me, the confession that he made next accurately defines the man he had become:

"…But as for me and my household, we will serve the Lord."
(Joshua 24:15, NIV)

That's the definition of a destiny statement. Joshua was a man who spent one-third of his life trying to figure out his purpose as God's servant. He had legitimate questions, and furthermore, legitimate struggle. The purpose God had for his life didn't come free of pain but wrapped in it. His humanity was obvious and his faith needed to be rehabilitated. But at the end of his life, when it was all said and done, it wasn't about the fame for God's army general. Nope! It was all about serving God. That was a decision that became concretized throughout Joshua's life. The very thing that was once a question was now a confession. Who was Joshua? Above everything else, he was a man who decided to serve God with everything inside of him.

I don't know the particulars of the pain and struggle of your story, but I do know that when you give your life to serve God with everything inside of you, He will fulfill the destiny of your life. Not only will you have the privilege of knowing God's love more fully, but your life will be a monument of that love for others who desperately need it.

Being the star of the show or having millions of followers on social media might create the allusion of success, and you might hope that success comes hand-in-hand with comfort and pleasure. But these things are far from the truth. True success is found in the authentic, gritty, and fully-committed confession: "As for me and my house, we will serve the Lord."

FINAL THOUGHTS

Before we come to a close, I want to specifically encourage the person who *has experienced* or *is experiencing* disruptions or dips. I wish I could look you in the eyes and tell you personally, but for now, this book will have to do. Here's what I want you to remember: it's not over. You're not dead, so God's not done. And because you still have a pulse, you still have a purpose.

Maybe you're going through a divorce. Maybe you just lost a child. Or you could be facing a prison sentence. You might have secrets that make you feel ashamed. You might believe God's mad at you and have given up on Him. Perhaps your world has been extremely dark because of anxiety and depression. Maybe you've even been contemplating throwing in the towel. This book was written to passionately implore you: **you better not give up!**

I don't know the specifics of your situation, but I do know the specifics of our God. What He did for Joshua, He will also do for you. How He turned my life around, He can turn yours around, too. If you surrender, your disruptions and dips will lead to God's destiny.

God is many things to us: a father, a protector, a warrior, and a friend. But one of my favorite things about Him lies within His creative capability. God is a masterful artist who calls us His masterpiece (Ephesians 2:10). But the artwork of our lives doesn't have a lavish, smooth, sleek, or perfect aesthetic.

There's a type of Japanese art known as *wabi-sabi,* or *the art of imperfection.* Legend states that a young man was asked to tend the garden of his revered master. The young man "cleaned up debris and raked the ground until it was perfect, then scrutinized the immaculate garden. Before presenting his work to the master, he shook a cherry tree, causing a few flowers to spill randomly onto the ground."[1]

The young man intuitively understood what many of us struggle to grasp: true beauty lies within imperfection. Real beauty isn't cleaned up perfectly and presented as a final product. Instead, real beauty is raw and real, imperfections and all.

It's no surprise that God understands this concept better than anybody. After all, He's in the business of using people like Joshua, myself, and you. The imperfection of your story is what points you and those around you to the perfection of God. He uses the backdrop of our struggle to bring out the beauty of our story.

THE IMPERFECTION OF YOUR STORY IS WHAT POINTS YOU AND THOSE AROUND YOU TO THE PERFECTION OF GOD.

There's nobody like our God! He's the only one that takes the calamity of our lives and turns it into a testimony that makes people say, "Your God is amazing!" He's the only one who can take multiple disruptions and dips to bring forth an even greater destiny. God scooped Joshua out of his extreme discouragement and restored everything that was promised to him. He's taken a broken man like me and transformed my life from ashes to beauty. And I *promise* you, He's writing your story in a way that is imperfect, yet breathtakingly beautiful.

For everyone who feels like the weight of your lifequake is crushing you, will you allow me to offer one final encouragement to you? Become a child again. Invite God, your Father, to scoop you up and rock you back and forth in His protective arms. Let Him speak to you in order to restore you.

You might be in the middle of some stuff that you didn't sign up for. But God can get you out of what life got you in. And furthermore, He will lead you to the destiny he has prepared for you.

REFLECTION & APPLICATION

1. When you think of your destiny, does it result in you serving people around you? If it doesn't, you may need to make some adjustments to the direction of your dreams.

2. How might God want to use your imperfection to magnify His perfection? Pray about how the things you have faced in the past and are facing in the present can draw others closer to God.

3. For everyone who is in the middle of a disruption or a dip, pray this prayer:

God, the Bible defines you as my Heavenly Father and says that I can call to you as Abba, or dad. Because of that, I come to you as a child and humbly ask for your grace in the middle of _____ (name your disruption or dip). Please, hold me in your arms, speak to me about my identity, and reassure me about my future. Give me endurance through this trial, and just like Joshua, give me the courage to march on toward destiny. I realize that I hold your light in a fragile jar of clay (2 Corinthians 4:7), and the perfection of your beauty shines through my imperfection. Therefore, I choose to praise you in the middle of my pain and believe that this process is developing me into the servant you've called me to be. In Jesus' name I pray, amen.

NOTES

Chapter One

1. Bruce Feiler, Life Is in the Transitions: Mastering Change at Any Age (New York, NY: Penguin Press, 2020).

Chapter Two

1. Kaiser, W. C. (1999). שׁמ1167. R. L. Harris, G. L. Archer Jr., & B. K. Waltke (Eds.), Theological Wordbook of the Old Testament (electronic ed., p. 496). Chicago: Moody Press.

Chapter Four

1. Queen, "I Want It All." The Miracle. Capitol, 1989.

2. A.W. Tozer, The Root of the Righteous: Tapping the Bedrock of True Spirituality (Camp Hill, PA: Wingspread, 2007).

Chapter Five

1. Feiler, Life Is in the Transitions.

2. Bruce Feiler, "The Stories That Bind Us," The New York Times. March 15, 2013. https://www.nytimes.com/2013/03/17/fashion/the-family-stories-that-bind-us-this-life.html

Chapter Six

1. "renew," Dictionary.com. March 12, 2021. https://www.dictionary.com/browse/renew

2. "apokalupsis," Biblehub.com. March 12, 2021. https://biblehub.com/greek/602.htm

3. Remez Sasson, "The Power of Repeated Words and Thoughts," Success Consciousness. 2001-2021. https://www.successconsciousness.com/blog/affirmations/the-power-of-repeated-words/

Chapter Seven

1. "Post-traumatic stress disorder," Mayoclinic.org. March 13, 2021. https://www.mayoclinic.org/diseases-conditions/post-traumatic-stress-disorder/symptoms-causes/syc-20355967

2. "rehab," Collins English Dictionary. March 13, 2021. https://www.collinsdictionary.com/dictionary/english/rehab

Chapter Ten

1. Robyn Griggs Lawrence, "Wabi-Sabi: The Art Of Imperfection," Utne Reader. September-October 2001. https://www.utne.com/mind-and-body/wabi-sabi#:~:text=Emerging%20in%20th e%20 15th%20century,of%20revering%20authenticity%20above%20all

Made in the USA
Middletown, DE
31 October 2021